C000255534

The Home Colours Sourcebook: Neutrals

The Home Colours Sourcebook: Neutrals

200 colour schemes for the home

Alice Buckley

APPLE

APPLE

A QUARTO BOOK

First published in the UK in 2008 by
Apple Press
7 Greenland Street
London NW1 0ND
United Kingdom
www.apple-press.com

Copyright © 2008 Quarto Publishing plc

All rights reserved. No part of this publication
may be reproduced, stored in a retrieval system, or transmitted in
any form or by any means, electronic, mechanical, photocopying,
recording or otherwise, without the permission of the copyright
holder.

ISBN: 978-1-84543-274-4

QUAR.NSB

Conceived, designed and produced by
Quarto Publishing plc.
The Old Brewery
6 Blundell Street
London N7 9BH

Project editor: Emma Poulter
Copy editor: Claire Waite Brown
Art director: Caroline Guest
Designer: James Lawrence
Proofreader: Ruth Patrick
Picture researcher: Sarah Bell
Indexer: Diana LeCore

Creative director: Moira Clinch
Publisher: Paul Carslake

Colour separation by Modern Age Repro
House Ltd., Hong Kong
Printed in China by Midas Printing
International Ltd.

10 9 8 7 6 5 4 3 2 1

Contents

About this book 6

Introduction 8

Neutrals through history 10

Colour theory 14

Colour and mood 16

Get inspired 18

Choosing your colour scheme 22

THE COLOUR PALETTE DIRECTORY

At a glance 28

Parisian elegance 32

Modern art 52

Stunning seascapes 76

Classic flora 96

Return to nature 116

Beauty of the desert 134

Moroccan dreams 152

Wilderness 170

Ice cream 192

Northern lights 214

White heat 232

Index 254

Credits 256

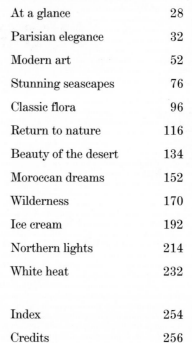

About this book

This book features 200 neutral colour schemes to inspire home decorators and interior designers. With useful information about the colours and the mood evoked by each, this is an invaluable resource that will help you to select a scheme and then create the perfect room, whether it be a warm and relaxing living room, a sexy, sumptuous bedroom or a light and airy kitchen.

The book begins with an introduction to neutrals – our perception of them, how they have been used throughout history, their influence and how they figure in the modern world. Once a brief overview has been established, the basic principles of colour theory are explained to provide you with a sound foundation from which to build upon.

While it is useful to have some understanding of colour principles, it is ultimately the relationship between these colours and the mood created by them that is important when implementing any interior scheme. The following pages discuss the different moods evoked by certain colour groups and how and where to get inspiration, before identifying the factors that influence our colour choices and why.

Neutrals are one of the easiest groups of colours to work with. They are extremely versatile and can be layered, mixed and matched. The final chapter, the colour palette directory, examines the huge array of neutral colours and combinations available, with ideas on all aspects of home decoration and furnishing, to help you create the perfect neutral interior.

Using the colour palettes

1 – Colour-coded bullets correspond to the colour chapter that you're in.

2 – Mood-enhancing words to help you imagine the feeling each scheme will evoke.

3 – The inspiration behind the scheme's colour choices.

4 – The theory behind the interior-design style. Find ideas and inspiration on materials and finishes, flooring, furniture, patterns and accessories.

5 – The main colour in the room, usually to be used on the walls, although sometimes furniture or flooring may be the main focus.

Take this book into your local DIY store and ask them to match a test pot to this colour. Paint a square of colour on your chosen area and let it dry, as paint always changes colour when it dries. Live with the colour for a day or two before committing to a whole room.

1

2

3

5

6

4

7

THE COLOUR PALETTE DIRECTORY

Rolling *landscapes*

Recreate the richness and vitality of the outdoors inside.

The region of Tuscany in central Italy is considered the birthplace of the Renaissance movement and has a rich artistic heritage. This scheme is reminiscent of the lush Italian landscape filled with cypress trees, olive groves and vineyards and soaked in glowing sunshine.

To conjure up the beauty of Tuscany, implement this palette in a lounge or dining room.

Cover the walls in baked clay (1) and add sofas upholstered in rich, velvety olive (4) with the odd statement chair in corn (2).

Put in a warm, natural oak floor with a couple of rugs in striped emerald grey (5) and Tuscan yellow (3).

Accessorize with cushions and vases or ceramic bowls in any one of these selected colours.

6 – Accent colours, which can be used for an adjacent wall, for woodwork or to match to upholstery fabrics. The colours may be darker or lighter tones of the main shade, shades to balance a room or complementary colours that create a contrast in your chosen interior.

7 – Each scheme also features two further highlight accent colours. These can take the form of a sharp injection of colour, such as a red vase in a very neutral pale blue interior, or the final balancing tone in a range of harmonious colours, such as a rich, chocolate brown in a room of soft, creamy toffee tones.

Although only used in small quantities, the highlight colours are often the most important shades of all, since they complete the design.

Introduction

"Home" is one of our most evocative words. It conjures up an image of warmth and shelter, of family and friends, a place of inspiration, sanctuary and peace. With so much that's important represented by this one place, it's no wonder that we're passionate about our homes and work to make them ever-more comfortable and welcoming.

Today's homes fulfil many functions beyond shelter and nurturing. We decorate our homes in ways that not only enable them to fulfil these needs but also to reveal our personalities, our aspirations, the very essence of ourselves and how we want others to see us. There are many ways of doing this. Among them are light and colour, two qualities that surround us in our natural environment, which can dramatically influence and alter our living space. With these two magic wands we can dictate the energy of a space, its mood and comfort level. If we use them well, light and colour can help us create a home that supplies the emotional and functional needs we look for in our homes and make them truly our own.

Understanding neutrals

Among the many colour palettes at our disposal, neutrals are probably the least understood. These colours are often dismissed as bland and nondescript, thought of as suitable only for hotels or homes about to go on the market, but neutrals have moved beyond those colours not found on the colour wheel, such as white, black, grey, brown and tan. The latest neutrals are sophisticated hints at gentle colour, and it's this subtlety that makes neutrals so exciting, versatile and effective.

Recent years have seen an emergence of a new crop of coloured neutrals. As we all strive for serenity within our homes, merging hints of colours that are muted and moody create new, fresh schemes. Deep and dark hues such as khaki, olive and steely grey through to the lighter pink beiges of taupe and mink all form part of the modern neutral palette. With a huge range of colour ideas, this book aims to help you make the most of neutrals in your interior scheme, and to achieve the mood or feeling you hope for in each room of your home.

USING TEXTURE

A skillfully constructed neutral interior crammed with texture and reflective pieces creates a sophisticated living space. Textured floor coverings and soft furnishings are pleasing to the eye and the touch, while the ceramics, Perspex table and feature mirror reflect and maximize the natural light.

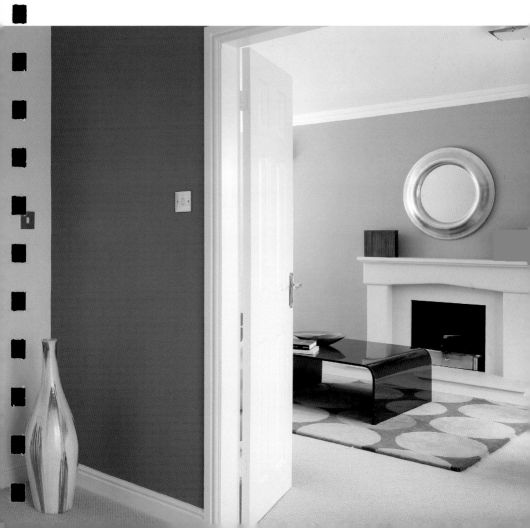

Neutrals through history

Cast away your preconceptions. Neutral isn't a euphemism for bland. The many tones and hues that fall into this category are an invitation to layering, contrast and texture. With or without an accent colour, neutrals can be as exciting as any scheme plucked from the colour wheel, yet they bring peace and serenity to our interiors and to our increasingly stressful lifestyles.

Choosing neutrals doesn't necessarily mean choosing contemporary. Many of the divergent decorative styles that evolved during the 20th century look sensational with neutral schemes. At the end of the Victorian age, art nouveau, whose sensuous, curvy lines are associated with muted, natural tones, was also the era of the architect and designer Charles Rennie Mackintosh, whose all white and black and white interiors still look cutting-edge today. The glamour and excitement of modernism, which took off in the 1920s, was an extraordinary display of innovative design—think black leather and chrome furniture set in sensational schemes of silver, black and white, and accessorized with fabulous animal prints.

Changing styles

Elegant art deco, with its stylized images and geometric shapes, was also at the height of its popularity during the 1920s and 1930s. It employed the same neutral schemes as modernism, as well as introducing elegant ivory and oyster alongside mother-of-pearl, polished and inlaid wood, black lacquer, stainless steel and startling black and white chequerboard linoleum floors. Shiny fabrics added texture and luxury to schemes that were monochrome yet mesmerizing. In Scandinavia, the

ORNATE ART NOUVEAU
The natural, flowing lines here are complemented by the glowing simplicity of rich cream studded with a jewel red accent. A complex palette of colours would make the scheme over busy and confusing.

CLASSICAL ARCHITECTURE
Striking architectural features in neutral stone,
marble and iron need little embellishment, though
the mood of the room can be dictated by different
styles of floral decoration.

ACCENTUATING ACCENTS

Never underestimate the importance of accent colours. Part of the beauty of a neutral colour scheme such as the one above, is that flashes of contrasting or bold colours can be included to bring a sense of fun into an otherwise utilitarian room.

1930s saw the emergence of a cool, pared-down, functional style with the accent on blond wood, natural materials, functional furniture and neutral tones from ecru to bright white with colour accents. Many of the designers prominent in this movement, including Arne Jacobsen and Alvar Aalto, are just as popular today. And, of course, Ikea promotes its own ubiquitous version of the look in its own style.

The postwar 1950s was the age of kitsch and bright Formica, yet ice-cream pastels, chrome appliances and design classics from the furniture studio of husband-and-wife team Charles and Ray Eames are perfect accessories for neutral schemes, as is the black and white op art of the flower-filled, colour-crazed 1960s.

Neutrals today

While neutrals can be adapted to most interior
schemes, that's not the only reason for their current
popularity. The wheel of fashion turns inexorably,
and it was inevitable that the bright colours and
busy schemes so popular in interiors of the 1980s
and early 1990s would give way to visually less
demanding interiors. In today's modern age,
neutrals in the home help to bring peace and calm
into our lives. Light and space, both of which can be
enhanced and maximized by the use of neutrals, are
vital factors for our well-being, and their importance
in our hectic lives should never be underestimated.

The glass lamp, with its delicate
lilac-grey shade, brings a surprising stab
of femininity to the dark forest green of
this rather masculine bedroom. The
texture of the cushions and bedspread
add interest to the neutral scheme.

Colour theory

A world without colour is unthinkable. From the glory of a landscape or the stunning plumage of a bird, to the wonder of a rainbow, a breathtaking flower or the food on our plates, colour enhances our lives. Understanding basic colour principles will turn your neutral scheme into a sensational interior.

Hering's colour wheel

Building upon Issac Newton's colour spectrum, the seven colours of the rainbow, and Thomas Young's discovery of the three primary colours that make up light—red, green and blue—Ewald Hering developed his own version of the colour wheel, giving yellow as the fourth "primary" colour. Yellow, he argued, ought to be a primary colour because it is seen by the eye as an independent hue, along with red, green and blue. He also included black and white as basic visual primary colours. Hering described his order of colours as "the natural system of colour sensations." Today, this system forms the basis of the Natural Colour System (NCS), which is used universally as a colour-matching tool.

HERING'S WHEEL
The four-colour primary wheel developed in 1878 by German physiologist Ewald Hering. The inner range of brown neutral colours has been added, within each of the 4 quadrants. These browns are created by mixing the four primaries in varying proportions.

ADDING WHITE
Using the Hering colour wheel as a basis, this wheel shows that by adding white, the resulting paler colours form a range of subtle tinted whites.

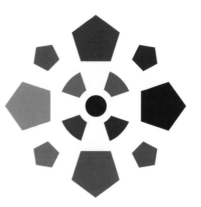

ADDING BLACK
By adding black, a range of darker neutral shades is achieved. With both these wheels, the same concepts of harmonious and complementary colours apply.

Harmonious colours

When the four pure "primary" colours of red, blue, green and yellow are mixed with their neighbours on the wheel, the secondary colours of purple, turquoise, orange and lime are produced. As you move around the wheel you can immediately see the harmonies between the adjacent colours. The same principles apply with neutrals—a soft buttermilk yellow will always work well with a burnt orange.

Complementary colours

These are the opposing colours on the wheel that vibrate against each other, or clash. Used cleverly in a scheme, these can be striking. Interestingly when two opposite complementary colours are mixed they make a neutral grey—this can be seen in the shadows cast from one colour onto its complement. The principle can be used in home decoration; if you are using two complements for paint work, try mixing them to make a third neutral colour, by definition it will link well into the two main colours.

Tonal colours

Choosing just one colour but using it in varying tones is a tonal or monochromatic scheme, and one that is very successful with neutrals. The addition of texture and pattern can help to bring tonal schemes to life but, remember, sticking to one single tone throughout does not constitute a neutral scheme and signs certain death for any interior.

Neutral colours

A neutral colour is one without any bias, and is difficult to achieve (and not necessarily desirable) when mixing paint or pigments. Even a true neutral grey when painted in a room, will take on the colours around it. Neutral colours are generally a mix of two to four primary colours that create a variety of greys and browns with the variation of white or black being added to make them into a tint or a shade.

COMPLEMENTARY SCHEMES
The daring scheme of complementary colours above works well thanks to neutral background shades, while the green mosaic of the bathroom below is enlivened by towels, which serve as colour accessories that can be changed to alter the mood of the room. Using a harmonious shade alongside the green, such as turquoise, would create an entirely different ambience.

Colour and mood

While our homes represent a place of sanctuary and contentment, each room fulfils a different function. The decorative scheme chosen for each should enhance its ability to fulfil that role, creating the perfect mood or atmosphere. Colour and light (both natural and artificial) are used to create the required ambience: an entrance hall, for instance, should be welcoming, a bedroom intimate and calm, while a dining room might project a mood of late-night sophistication.

Different colour groups create different moods and emotions. Neutrals, however, are just as able to determine the mood of a room, particularly when used with texture and an accent colour. For instance, if sunflower yellow is perfect for an entrance hall, a cheery butter beige in a neutral scheme will produce the same welcoming mood, while red-toned neutrals will create a stunning ambience in a dining room. The mood enhancing properties of colours are just as accessible in a thoughtful neutral scheme.

Mood and function

Does it make you smile, shiver or sigh with contentment? It's well known that certain colour groups inspire particular moods and lend themselves to being used in particular rooms. While the amount of colour used or the depth of the tone may alter the impact, the general principle remains, even in a neutral scheme in which the tone will be subdued or the colour used purely as an accent.

A HARMONIOUS SCHEME
Cheerful yet calm, the harmonious greens, yellows and creams of this kitchen work beautifully to create an easy and attractive scheme.

Pinks: Feminine, frothy, fun and happy. A favourite for girls' bedrooms, pinks are also great in drawing and sitting rooms. For neutrals, use candy pink tones or the palest apple blossom.

Reds: Passionate, racy, warm and comforting. Red is the colour of life, perfect for reception rooms and dining rooms. For neutrals, make it dark and rich, with the deepest tones of ripe plum or burgundy.

Oranges: Stimulating, fun and warm. Orange is a contradiction, depending on both the shade and its use. Team it with yellow tones to join the wide-awake club or with soft ochres and blues for a Mediterranean dream. For neutrals, stick to burnt oranges and muted tones.

Yellows: Happy, sunny and mellow. Yellow offers a cheery welcome. Not recommended for bedrooms. For neutral variations of this shade, try butter beiges and lemon creams.

Greens: Natural, easy and peaceful. Nature's favourite colour works just about anywhere. In a neutral scheme, implement a deep sage or olive green or a greyed basil green.

Blues: Cool, calm, clear and relaxing. The colour of sky and water, blue needs good light to look its best. Think pale blues for bathrooms and bedrooms and deeper, greyish tones for dining rooms.

Violets: Pretty, powerful and regal. Use violets with care. Paler shades work in most situations, but save deep, rich violets for sexy bedrooms.

Browns: Rich, warm, earthy colours. Think of the inspirational Italian pigments of sienna, umber, ochre or terracotta, and use with the greys and rusty iron colours of natural slate tiles.

Grays: In its purest form, grey is the nearest to the ultimate neutral, as it contains no colour, and so acts as a good foil for other brighter colours. Choose from neutral pale dove grey to rich dark charcoal grey, or a grey with a hint of colour, such as a velvety mouse grey or a cool Smokey Mountain grey.

COMBINING BRIGHTS AND LIGHTS
The bold reds and pinks of this scheme are neutralized somewhat by the presence of white, resulting in a more balanced room.

Get inspired

The world around us is buzzing with inspiration for neutral schemes. Whether you're in the city, by the sea or in the country, whatever the season and weather and be it natural wonders or man-made works, take a moment to look objectively at anything and everything that catches your eye. Look at the subtle colours of tree bark, from silver birch to dappled limes, the moody greys and pinks of storm clouds, oyster shells with a wedge of bright lemon, a cityscape reflected in a river and the myriad shades in a chunk of stone or a handful of pebbles.

For another perspective, look at these same colour themes through the eyes of the masters. How have they been used and interpreted by artists through the ages, by Vermeer, Picasso, Miro, Nash? What is it about one store window, fashion plate or advertisement that draws you while another leaves you cold? You don't have to be an artist yourself to find a palette that pleases you and creates the mood you hope to reproduce in your home.

Using scrapbooks

It's never too soon to start gathering ideas and pasting them into a scrapbook. Packaging, magazine pages featuring anything from fashion and interiors to food and flowers, posters, paint cards, flyers, postcards, birthday cards, holiday snaps, even a photograph of the amazing mix of colours in the coat of a leopard or your pet dog. If you like it, paste it in. Stills from favourite television programmes and films are fertile ground. Period dramas, expertly researched and true to their era, are rich with inspiration, but so is contemporary film with lavish locations dressed by the world's best stylists. Model your scheme on *The Godfather*'s Sicilian villa or a seascape from *Message in a Bottle*. As your book fills,

GENERATING IDEAS
Little bits of what you like will fill your head with ideas and help you to bring together the perfect scheme. These ideas point towards a mix of rich, warm, earthy neutrals balanced with pattern, a little shine and perhaps a splash of accent colour.

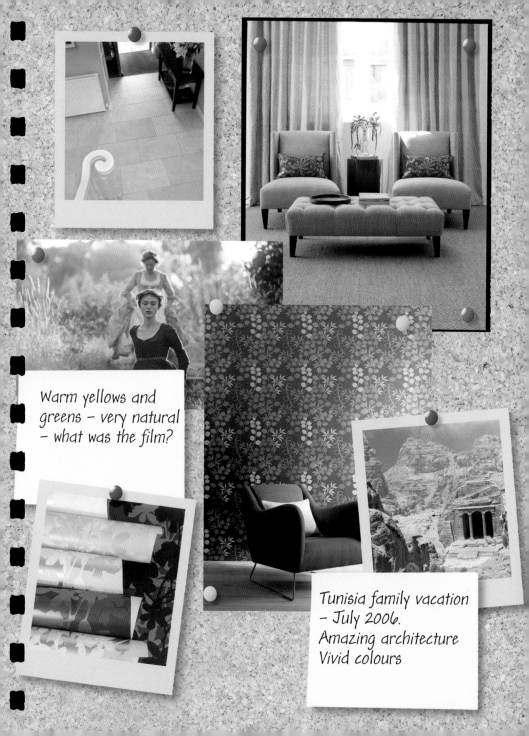

Warm yellows and greens – very natural – what was the film?

Tunisia family vacation – July 2006. Amazing architecture Vivid colours you'll see a theme developing. Viewing the world with interested eyes will make every trip, however mundane, a journey of discovery.

Moodboards

Once you know what you like, create a moodboard. A tool used by designers, a moodboard is the distillation of your chosen colours, textures and fabrics. If your scheme has to include something that you won't be changing, such as a carpet or a stone fireplace, include it on the board. If you're building a scheme from scratch, begin compiling the board around your main colour. Or you may want to base the scheme around an inspirational starting point, such as a favourite rug or painting, and pick your colours from that piece. Include paint swatches and fabric samples: the moodboard isn't just about colour but also pattern and texture.

To give as true a representation as possible, place the carpet swatch or wood/tile sample at the bottom of the board, soft furnishing swatches in the centre, curtain swatches at the side and paint swatches as appropriate. If your accent colour is going to cover a whole wall, it should feature prominently on the moodboard. If it will be no more than a pair of cushions, make it proportionally smaller. Anything that disrupts the harmony of the scheme should be removed, no matter how much you like it—you can always use it in another room.

SECONDARY SOURCES
The great artists understood colour, so don't be afraid to steal themes, ideas and inspiration from their work to incorporate into your own schemes. These rich reds, golds and browns balanced by palest pink, fawn and cream will create a warm, restful scheme perfect for a sitting room or bedroom.

Cushions at mum's

I love this picture by Vermeer – rich colours. Could it work in my house?

I remember the trees on the lake in autumn —those golden browns, are so beautiful – study colour?

Choosing your colour scheme

As your neutral scheme takes form there are several influential factors to be considered before you reach for the paintbrush or order your fabric. Mood, function, light and flow must all play a part in your decisions if your scheme is to be a success.

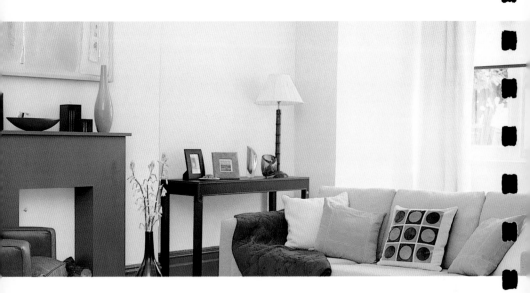

PERFECT HARMONY
Dark wood furniture loses definition in a dark room, but these wonderful chocolate shades are brought to life by creamy walls, while the tall windows, cleverly curtained with pale fabric and blinds, flood the room with flattering natural light that accentuates each shade of fabric and piece of furniture.

The importance of light

Light is the giver of life, not just for the world in general, but also for your scheme and the mood it creates. Get it wrong and your interior will look dull and flat. Get it right and your scheme will glow with balance and harmony. Abundant natural light is on the wish list of every home owner, and, as one of the most influential factors in the success or failure of your interior, it's worth maximizing available natural light with gauzy fabrics, glass, mirrors and light-reflecting colours. In this respect, neutrals are no different to primary colours: lighter shades reflect light and darker ones absorb it.

Natural light: Natural light shows neutrals at their best, but all schemes will be affected by the time of day, the sun's aspect and the quality of the light as the seasons change. If possible, use south-facing rooms during the day so that you can make the most of available light, and perhaps make a north-facing room the dining room, which will be used mostly at night. Warming shades, often used in dining rooms, will also go some way to making up for the colder light of a north-facing aspect.

Artificial light forms: Artificial light can be unkind to colour, so it needs to be used thoughtfully. There are three main lighting styles to choose from: task, ambient and mood. Task lighting is strong and direct and used for reading, cooking or other work. Ambient supplies general illumination, but avoid overhead lighting – the ubiquitous pendant hanging from the centre of the ceiling is harsh and unflattering and makes colours look flat. (Chandeliers, which throw sensational, diffused light, are excluded from this rule.)

Lamps and wall lighting are kinder and more versatile. You can also light for mood, creating atmosphere, usually intimate and romantic, which is ideal for bedrooms and dining rooms. Fluorescent light is tricky. If you don't really need it give it a miss, even in kitchens.

Importantly, all artificial light alters colour. To make sure your colour choices work, test them by painting a paper or plasterboard sample (do not paint directly onto the walls) and placing it in various positions in the room, in various lights, before committing yourself.

Flow

To aid flow throughout the house, one idea is to choose a main colour and use it in each room as the basis for individual schemes, possibly on the walls but alternatively on the floor or the skirting boards.

MODERN DESIGN
Contemporary open-plan homes, which often have mainly white or all-white interiors (as shown above and below), are usually designed with a generous use of glass to supply masses of natural light. The double height of the living area also adds to the abundance of light and the feeling of space.

If you choose a tonal scheme, using several shades of one main colour, use the lightest shade on the ceiling, the middle shade on the walls and the darkest shade on the lower half of the wall – if you have a dado rail – or on the floor where appropriate. Also consider the type of paint you will be using: at its simplest, the various grades of gloss will reflect light and therefore look lighter than matte.

Texture and pattern

Texture, another important factor in a neutral scheme, not only adds visual and tactile interest but also contributes to the overall mood of a room. One of the joys of a neutral scheme is the fun you can have with texture, from woven natural fibres on the floor and faux fur throws on the sofa or bed to piles of cushions in appliqué, pleated silk, fluffy wool or studded with decorative buttons.

OLD MEETS NEW
The restful sage green of the tongue and groove balanced with cream creates a traditional neutral scheme in this bathroom, though modern fixtures give it a pleasing contemporary edge.

COOLING COLOURS
Reminiscent of New England or Scandinavia,
this kitchen's magical, delicate combination
of shades of grey, green and white speak of
the cool light of the northern hemisphere.
The room's obvious functionality makes it
welcoming and pleasant to be in.

Textured components will be more noticeable in a neutral scheme, than any other, so be sure to choose things that you truly like.

Pattern also comes into its own in a neutral scheme. If you choose to have just one pattern in a room's scheme you can afford to go large, perhaps papering one wall with a fabulous bold pattern, possibly in an eye-catching feature colour. Shiny materials, such as chrome, steel, black lacquer and marble, also introduce excitement and interest into the calm of a neutral scheme.

Colour considerations

Planning one neutral room in a home otherwise filled with colour is perfectly possible, so long as the adjacent rooms, visible when the doors are open, don't start a screaming match. A scarlet dining room, for instance, will sit comfortably next to a neutral sitting room if a red-toned neutral or a red accent is part of the scheme, even if only a small part. The same floor treatment running throughout will also unify rooms. Colours in adjacent rooms must always be taken into account.

If you're decorating your home in order to sell it, keep your scheme simple. Sometimes a striking, off-the-wall interior will sell a house, but it's more likely to limit your pool of potential purchasers, whereas a discreet scheme will make them feel comfortable and able to move in, even if it's not completely to their taste.

As you make decisions about the components of your neutral scheme, don't forget another important factor—yourself. Choose shades, colours and fabrics that work but also that you enjoy. There's no single "correct" scheme. If you can stick to the basic rules, combine your likes and avoid dislikes, you'll end up with a beautiful interior that's a pleasure to live in.

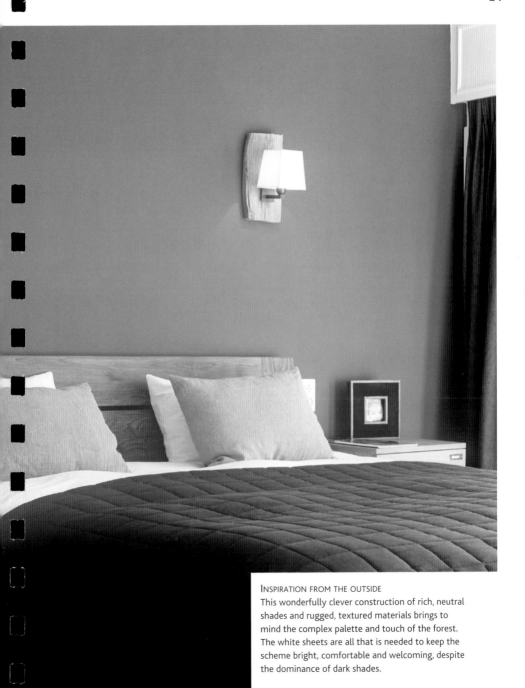

Inspiration from the outside
This wonderfully clever construction of rich, neutral shades and rugged, textured materials brings to mind the complex palette and touch of the forest. The white sheets are all that is needed to keep the scheme bright, comfortable and welcoming, despite the dominance of dark shades.

The Colour Palette Directory

THIS EASY-TO-USE CHART ILLUSTRATES THE MAIN COLOUR IN EACH OF THE 200 PALETTES. YOU CAN SELECT A COLOUR THEN TURN TO THE CORRECT PAGE AND DISCOVER HOW TO USE IT EFFECTIVELY IN A PARTICULAR ROOM SCHEME.

34–35 36–37 38–39

40–41 42-43 44–45

46–47 48–49 50-51

54–55 56–57 58–59

60–61 62–63 64–65

66–67 68–69 70–71

72–73 74–75 78–79

80–81

82–83

84–85

86–87

88–89

90–91

92–93

94–95

98–99

100–101

102–103

104–105

106–107

108–109

110–111

112–113

114–115

118–119

120–121

122–123

124–125

126–127

128–129

130–131

132–133

136–137

138–139

140–141

142–143

144–145

146–147

148–149

150–151

154–155

156–157

158–159

160–161

162–163

164–165

166–167

168–169

172–173

174–175

176–177

178–179

180–181

182–183

184–185

186–187

188–189

190–191

194–195

196–197

198–199

200–201

202–203

204–205

206–207

208–209

210–211

212–213

216–217

218–219

220–221

222–223

224–225

226–227

228–229

230–231

234–235

236–237

238–239

240–241

242–243

244–245

246–247

248–249

250–251

252–253

Parisian elegance

Our opening chapter creates sophistication and glamour with colour. Long envied as a regal shade, mauve encompasses warm lilacs and subtle lavenders. Think of art deco glamour, tea rooms with white china and martinis served in cut crystal. Adorn your home with decadent textures of velvet and silk and embellished furnishings in classic styles.

Paradise *found*

Rich, intense hues are complemented by nature's neutrals.

Deep plum is a rich and evocative interior colour that can add depth and mood to an enclosed or dark space. Warm, passionate and intense, this ripe colour makes a great shade for an extravagant feature wall, particularly in a dining room or romantic bedroom.

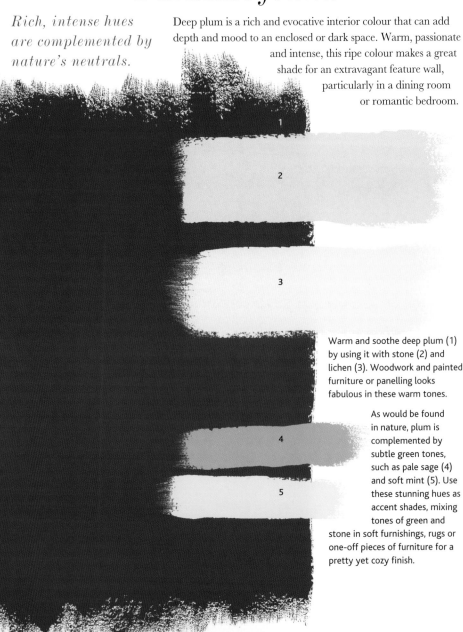

Warm and soothe deep plum (1) by using it with stone (2) and lichen (3). Woodwork and painted furniture or panelling looks fabulous in these warm tones.

As would be found in nature, plum is complemented by subtle green tones, such as pale sage (4) and soft mint (5). Use these stunning hues as accent shades, mixing tones of green and stone in soft furnishings, rugs or one-off pieces of furniture for a pretty yet cozy finish.

Paradise *lost*

Layering deep tones of petrol blue and deep plum is a brave scheme to take on, but, if used thoughtfully, accent accessories – whether soft furnishings, ceramics or artwork – in dramatic, sensuous petrol blue complement this shade of plum beautifully and will result in a striking room.

Perfect for a cozy lounge, snug or hideaway or a glamorous dining room.

Paint all walls in deep plum (1), woodwork in light grey (3) and even consider painting the floor or using light grey as a carpet colour to contrast with the richness of the plum. Panther grey (2) would work for sofas or throws in a snug or as a large, centralized rug in a dining room.

Mix petrol blue (4) and charcoal (5) in curtaining and other soft furnishings. These tones lend themselves well to glamorous and sumptuous fabrics such as leather, velvet and silks.

Moulin *rouge*

A deep, delicious and decadently girly group of colours.

This combination is reminiscent of the glory days of the Moulin Rouge, where dancers in deep amethyst silk dresses flaunted themselves and cavorted together through the night. The palette captures much of the romance of early 20th century France that was evident in the club's decor.

1

2

3

4

5

Amethyst (1) is a deep, regal shade. Use it on bedroom walls for a sensual room, with curtains or drapes of fabric in deep purple (5). Use pretty pinks, like blush (2) and candy (3), for bed linen and accessories.

To bring elegance to the look of the room, paint furniture and woodwork in mushroom (4), which looks best in a matte finish. You could also use mushroom for an accent wall if amethyst is too overpowering for the whole room.

Finally, bring deep purple back into the room in an accent piece, be that a throw for the bed or a single upholstered chair.

Powder *room*

This playful collection of colours are inspired by the fun and glamour of the 1950s. The cosmetic-coloured accents work well with the depth of the amethyst, and successfully complement juicy plum and the warm brown of deep chestnut. This scheme works well in a lounge or snug as well as a bedroom.

A vintage palette inspired by the 1950s.

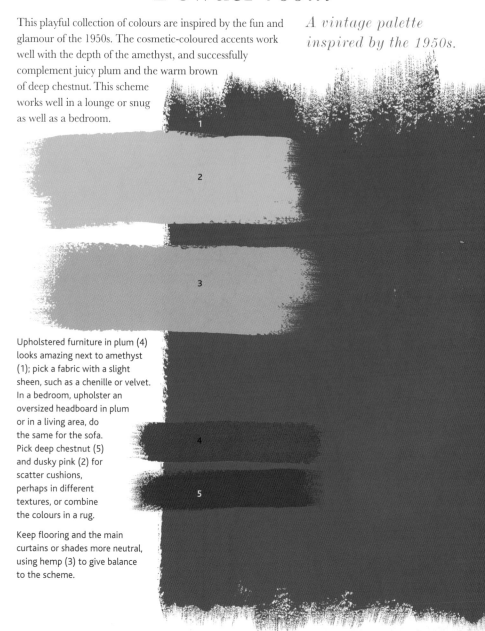

Upholstered furniture in plum (4) looks amazing next to amethyst (1); pick a fabric with a slight sheen, such as a chenille or velvet. In a bedroom, upholster an oversized headboard in plum or in a living area, do the same for the sofa. Pick deep chestnut (5) and dusky pink (2) for scatter cushions, perhaps in different textures, or combine the colours in a rug.

Keep flooring and the main curtains or shades more neutral, using hemp (3) to give balance to the scheme.

Understated *elegance*

Embrace the beauty of Art Nouveau with these fresh colours.

The Art Noveau movement, like many design styles, sought to harmonize its forms, and this colour scheme seeks to do the same. The fresh, subtle tints of this palette are perfect for a stylish entrance hall or a light, bright drawing room.

1

2

3

Panelling looks fabulous in a hallway, especially when painted in heritage cream (2). Use dusk (1) as a richer complementary wall colour above the panelling for a striking effect.

Incorporate slate (4) into the soft furnishings, and experiment with texture, perhaps with some full-length silk curtains, highlighted with warm sand (5) and fresh green (3) in the details or accessories, such as fringes, cushions or vases.

5

Architectural *influence*

This serious, contemporary palette is crying out for a modern apartment or beautifully proportioned Georgian house – these timeless colours will work well in almost any room. Take inspiration from architectural elements, such as truffle grey and dark steel.

A masculine, pared-down, but highly sophisticated colour story.

1

2

3

Paint the walls in dusk (1). For a softer and warmer feel, use rose-cream (4) as the colour for flooring.

Upholster furniture in truffle grey (5), using a rich chenille or velvet for a striking and bespoke look and a luxurious texture.

Add high gloss or painted furniture in steel (2) or truffle grey, and use all tones, including silver-stone (3), in curtains, blinds, cushions and rugs.

4

5

Elegant *cosmo style*

Team neutrals with mauves for a warm and inviting scheme.

Keep things simple and grown-up with rich toffee and chocolate colours mixed with muted mauves. The delicious, creamy feel of this colour combination will help you to create a sumptuous, relaxed feel, perfect for a beautiful bedroom or cozy living area.

1

2

3

Intensify the beauty of mink (1) walls with furniture in walnut or wengé or painted in warm tones of bitter chocolate (5). If using this scheme in a bedroom, inject some drama by painting a feature wall behind the bed in damson (4) or use it as an upholstery fabric for a large, deluxe headboard.

4

5

Khaki (2) and eggshell (3) are beautiful neutrals that can be mixed in using cotton or linen bedding and soft accessories. Use natural floor coverings such as coir or seagrass in khaki to give this scheme a colonial edge.

Art *Nouveau*

The Art Nouveau movement in architecture and design used highly stylized, organic forms as inspiration. In furniture, architecture, art and everyday design, hues from all aspects of nature were used. A calming and soothing tone, mink is reminiscent of the Art Nouveau period.

A sophisticated look that remains pretty and delicate.

1

2

3

Fabrics in pink clay (4) and deep lavender (5), used to upholster furniture and for curtains in a large drawing room or open-plan living space, will tone beautifully with mink (1) coloured walls. Against this backdrop, paint cupboards, woodwork or shelving in limestone (2), which would also work well as a painted floor or carpet.

4

5

Accessorize with cushions in limestone (2), perhaps in silk or chenille fabric, and large ceramic bowls or artworks in heather (3) and deep lavender.

Stimulating, *warm and sensual*

Stunning colours for a grand entrance or impressive staircase.

Mention the word French grey and you are thrown into an elegant mindset; imagine lounging on a chaise longue, drinking a martini served in a beautiful cut-crystal glass. French grey works just about anywhere, but these selected colours are perfect for an entrance hall.

1

2

3

To give an old staircase a new lease on life, paint the spindles, treads and risers in ivory (2), but define the handrail in a deeper colour, such as mushroom (3), or a real wood finish, such as oak. Add a runner to the stairs in a stripe that combines mushroom (3) deep lilac (4) and gorgeous raspberry (5).

4

5

Paint chairs and picture rails in French grey (1), as well as the walls for maximum contemporary glamour. Add curtains, cushions and other accessories in any combination of the palette's five colours.

Grown-up *opulence*

The glamour and impact of this scheme is destined for a super-modern kitchen or open-plan living space, however, the palette would also translate into a bedroom setting. In an open-plan, contemporary conversion or new build you should have fun with colour and not be afraid to go for it.

Uncompromised luxury, full of tactile experiences and fabrics.

For ultimate impact against the warmth of French grey (1), put in a kitchen with cupboards and units finished in high-gloss purple (3) and sleek and shiny black (4) granite worktops. Silver grey (5) accessories and appliances and other utilitarian items in chrome will zing the colours to life.

In a living area, choose simple stripes or bold patterns in bitter chocolate (2) and purple for soft furnishings, with a background or base colour of French grey.

Evening *promise*

Masculine colours with feminine undertones.

Masculine meets feminine and warm meets cool in this scheme, yet while the cool tones of royal navy and steel blue contrast with the warmer components of the palette, all seem to work in harmony. This moody and subtle selection would suit a study or drawing room.

1

2

3

Paint the walls in graceful heather (1) for a beautiful base from which to work.

Subdue the pinky purple highlights of heather with heavy, full-length drapes in dark stone (2) and steel blue (3), and use either steel blue or dark stone as the main upholstery fabric for sofas or chairs. Accessorize using royal navy (5) and steel blue vases and lamp bases.

4

5

Use pale lilac (4) and heather for cushions and throws to lift the scheme.

Mineral *spa*

Well known were the healing and healthful benefits of spas to those wealthy enough to take respite in them in the late 19th and early 20th centuries. The colours of natural minerals in rock and crystal forms vary greatly – take inspiration from these and create your own spa.

Light some candles, run a bath and take time to relax.

1

2

3

Paint bathroom walls in heather (1) and tongue and groove and bathroom furniture in rich, warm mulberry (5) or fresh, calming marble (3).

Use mulberry and blueberry (4) as inspirational colours for tiles. For a more subtle scheme, you could look at natural slate. Use mirrors to capitalize on any natural light.

4

5

Decorate the bathroom by adding accessories and thick, fluffy towels in refreshing marble and sulphur blue (2).

Grecian *inspired*

Bold blue details to brighten a neutral kitchen.

Early 20th-century fashion designer Mariano Fortuny's "Delphos" dresses were inspired by Ancient Greek clothing and drapery. Made from finely pleated silk, his designs and the simplicity of his style were hugely popular with the rich artistic elite of the day, and this scheme pays homage to him.

1

2

3

4

5

Use this wonderful colour combination to adorn your kitchen or dining room. Use soft iris (1) for the majority of your kitchen units, but if you have a larger kitchen paint a stand-alone or island unit in subtle marble (2). Add worktops in mid-oak (3). Paint the largest feature wall in dusty blue (5) and the rest in subtle marble.

If you have space, include a mid-oak dining table and match with petrol blue (4) upholstered chairs. Don't forget about the finer details of dinnerware: mix different serving dishes in soft iris, dusty blue and subtle marble.

La *Belle Époque*

French for "the beautiful era" the late 19th-century movement of Belle Époque was ostentatious and for the wealthy. All about decadence, it presented a plethora of decorative accessories, such as delicate parasols, feathered hats and beautiful ribboned gloves.

A period of affluence and accessories reborn in this scheme.

1

2

3

For a truly beautiful bedroom, paint walls in soft iris (1). Choose French-boudoir-style furniture painted in rich cream (2). Go for fancy scrolling Baroque beds and perfectly formed armoires, because the intense detail of this style of furniture will look classic and understated when painted. Upholster the headboard or cover a chaise longue in dusky pink (3) and blueberry (4), and include fern (5) for cushions and accessories.

4

5

This scheme can be made lighter by painting the flooring in rich cream or richer by carpeting the floor in blueberry.

Dynamic *deco glamour*

Art Deco style: elegant, functional and, above all, modern.

This glamorous movement was the birthplace of Modernism. Opulent and lavish, art deco was an amalgamation of styles – details were geometric and images stylized. Inspired by the essence of this movement, this scheme is suited to an open-plan living space with high ceilings and architectural details.

1

2

3

Use mauve (1) to cover walls in an open living space. Offset mauve's delicate colour with masculine greens and greys. Metal finishes such as chrome and steel played a big part in Deco design. Use steel blue (2) for furniture and chrome for any metal detailing.

Create a striking geometric fireplace or add furniture tops in marble (3).

4

5

Add statement pieces of furniture in bold purple (5) and muted jade blue (4).

Vintage *style*

Vintage styles constantly evolve and grow, so always keep an eye out for one-off pieces of pretty vintage fabric, statement pieces of furniture or interesting prints or pictures. Combine various colours and textures, pattern with plain, silk with cotton and wood with mirror and plastic.

A subdued palette with a selection of your favourite vintage pieces.

1

2

3

Paint walls in mauve (1) and carpet or paint floors a shade darker in purple flora (2). Pick taupe (4) as the main colour for curtains or the largest items of furniture, and charcoal (5) for other pieces. Choose good-quality, tactile fabrics for furniture and curtains—they have to feel luxurious to stop a vintage scheme looking shabby rather than chic.

4

5

Add striped rugs and throws in buttermilk (3) and purple flora to complete the look.

Pretty *in pink*

Soft pink tones perfect for a girl's bedroom.

Pink can be overpowering used to excess, but it makes for a beautiful, almost fragrant bedroom when thoughtfully combined with these accent colours. Straight off the cosmetic counter, these playful pinks and violets cry out to be used in a girl's bedroom.

1

2

3

Paint the walls in pinked grey (1). Pick out fixed features, such as a fireplace or fitted wardrobes, in milkshake (3).

For the windows, use coffee (4) shades and delicate flowing voiles or silks as drapes in petal (2) and gorgeous pansy pink (5).

4

5

It's all about the details when you're being girly, so add crystal handles and decorative accessories in pansy pink. Flooring can be pure white floorboards or, for a warmer feel, carpet in coffee.

Timeless *romance*

Take inspiration from the pretty colours of makeup, but refine the pinks and purples into muted pinky greys and neutrals. Use bold reds and pinks and purples to accent the scheme, be that with artwork, a single vase or a simple, bold cushion.

A more mature palette for a romantic yet contemporary look.

1

2

3

Complementing pinked grey (1) walls, paint or paper a feature wall in lavender (3).

Keep sofas and chairs to a neutral grey (2) in a simple woven, textured fabric.

Add lamps and diffused lighting with simple glass bases and shades in either lavender, or pinked grey.

4

5

Use chalky coral (4) and/or oxblood (5) in a one-off canvas, floor vase or single chair to set the scheme off.

Modern art

Flirting between cooler blue-greys, greens
and warm stony neutrals, grey is a moody
contemporary tone. Associate these palettes with
geometric shapes, steel, glass and metal. Highlight
muddy creams, murky whites and gritty greys with
hints of rich pigments or acid brights. Use these
pages to conjure up images of modern interiors,
utilitarian and functional in style.

Primary *modern*

Take on Mondrian's lines in a bold, fun playroom.

The great French painter Piet Mondrian is synonymous with the concept of primary colours with black. His paintings of straight black lines and "pods" of red, yellow and blue have been replicated in design and interiors many times. Use this colour selection to interpret the style in your own way.

Paint opposing walls or panels on walls in a combination of primary red (2), bright yellow (3) and blue (4). Mask out lines in coal black (1) to separate the colour panels. Put a practical rubber floor down in coal black and punctuate this with small rugs in the three primary colours.

To keep the look fresh and clean, paint skirting boards and ceilings in pure white (5). As an added treat for the children, paint reachable rectangular squares with blackboard paint.

Lively *simple lines*

The modern artist Wassily Kandinsky was obsessed with colour and form, and his abstract paintings from the early part of the 20th century are lively explosions of colourful abstracts. His shapes and colours interject and overlap in a very free and almost haphazard way.

Layer a muted palette of greys and ochres for a luxurious bedroom.

Coordinate the furniture in the bedroom from the bed to the wardrobe doors in coal black (1) gloss or black glass. Paint the walls in chalk (3) and carpet the floor in rich yellow ochre (2). If you can find a good retro wallpaper with ochres, purples and blacks, use this to paper the bed-side wall of the room. Upholster the headboard in decadent coal black silk, with chalk silk buttoning.

Finally, layer decorative bedding in shades of yellow ochre, verde (4) and purple (5).

Punchy *pop art*

Be inspired by the
Swinging Sixties.

Synonymous with the new, exciting and radical trends of the time, this 1960s palette is based around bold and bright hues. These punchy colours would translate well in a large, high-ceilinged room.

1

2

3

Paint the largest wall of the room in minted white (2) to give a focal point and the rest of the walls in pure white (3), and then choose a carpet, wood floor or rubber floor in charcoal (1).

4

Add bold pieces of furniture in sunset orange (4) and other smaller items, such as cushions or vases, in pale lilac (5).

5

Finally, accessorize the white walls by adding pop art prints on canvas to bring the whole scheme together.

Artist's *studio*

If you've ever been lucky enough to see an artist at work, you'll know they have palettes, jars, half-finished paintings and brushes everywhere. It's organized chaos, but a cozy and welcoming space.

A neutral base is a blank canvas to work within.

1

2

3

Recreate an artist's paradise using found objects and quirky antique pieces of furniture.

Use charcoal (1) for the walls in a cozy sitting room, and carpet the floor in creamy buff (2).

Add different wood finishes, such as dark and medium oak (5, 4), for example, with furniture and picture frames. You may also want to add a framed mirror in the same wood finish. Moss green (3) makes an excellent choice for upholstered chairs and other soft furnishing items.

4

5

Making *an impression*

*Use colour freely
and embrace
Impressionism.*

The late 19th-century Impressionist art movement that began in Paris changed the face of painting forever. Characterized by ordinary scenes as subject matter, visible brushstrokes, unusual visual angles and an emphasis on light and its changing qualities, it was at one with nature.

1

2

3

This pretty palette of soft, timeless accents will work in many applications but would be perfect for a kitchen.

Make your worktops and wall tiles granite (1), and complement them with ash white (2) painted cupboards and ceramic crackle-glaze knobs in morning blue (5). Hints of this blue will lift colour from the granite.

4

5

For the ceiling and remaining woodwork use pure white (3), and paint the remaining wall space in lavender white (4). Accessorize with dinnerware in any of these colours.

Painting *the weather*

The great British artist Joseph William Turner painted spectacular recreations of natural weather conditions, such as sunlight, storms, rain and fog. There is such a depth of colour in his work; even in his scenes of shipwrecks and storms there are pockets of pinks, oranges and bright blues.

Use Turner's moody colours in the hallway of a traditional house.

Interpret Turner's style in your own way to create a stunning entrance and hallway.

Use a natural stone or slate floor in granite (1) through the entrance and hall of your house. Paint blue slate (4) below the dado rail and lighter natural stone (3) above it.

Paint skirting boards and woodwork in white stone (2), and carpet the stairs with a runner in salmon pink (5) for a splash of colour. Alternatively, inject this colour by adding the odd picture frame or vase in the same shade.

Restrained *fresco detailing*

A blush palette of plaster-inspired colours.

Painting frescoes is a highly skilled and difficult job. Many of the greatest paintings in Europe, such as the ceiling of the Sistine Chapel, are decorated in frescoes. Painted on a thin layer of wet plaster, pigments sink into this layer so that the plaster itself becomes the medium.

1

2

3

This plaster-inspired scheme is perfect for a bedroom or lounge.

Use panther grey (1) as a base colour for furniture; this could be painted flat or as a contemporary greyed-oak finish or used to paint walls. Alternatively, paint walls in plaster (4) for a warm pink glow and woodwork in oyster (2) for a subtle tonal difference.

4

5

Upholster furniture in minky brown (3) velvet or silk, and find a simple but elegant patterned fabric for curtains or blinds in a mix of Venetian pink (5) and minky brown.

Wild *Fauvism*

Inspired by the French word *fauve*, meaning "wild animals," the Fauvists went wild with colour. Fauvism progressed from Impressionism, with simplified designs in bright colours, characterized by artists such as Henri Matisse and Raoul Dufy.

Blues and purples feature heavily in the Fauvists' colourful paintings.

Use bold colour washes, as Dufy did, in a grown-up lounge. Use panther grey (1) as the wall colour, bar one, which will form the backdrop of the scheme. Cover this wall in panels of lavender (3) silk. Carpet the lounge in white lilac (2), using a carpet with silk or a slight sheen running through it if possible.

Frame the entrance to the lounge and any external windows or glass doors with tall, elegant planters in deep ocean (5), planted with simple structural plants or cacti. Curtain with full-length silks that pool on the carpet in Chinese blue (4) and lavender.

Drawing *the outside in*

A combination of colours based on the great outdoors.

In the 1880s, large numbers of British artists began to visit Cornwall in England, and the pretty fishing village of Newlyn soon became home to a school of artists, who started the "plein air" movement. Translating as "open air", it encouraged artists to paint outdoors.

1

2

3

The silvery undertones in buttercup cream (2) will complement a lead (1) carpet or natural stone floor. Use it as your wall colour, and team with sackcloth (5) as a woven, heavy linen for curtains, with pastel white (4) sheer beneath.

4

Choose sackcloth cotton or chenille as upholstery fabric for luxurious sofas, and add plenty of scatter cushions in duck egg (3), in different textures.

5

Natural, *organic arrangement*

Sculptural forms can be simply beautiful. From Henry Moore's huge abstractions of organic shapes to a tiny Art Deco nude bronze. A sculpture is a piece to be admired in its own right. With this in mind, this palette would suit a room for an indoor pool, where the main focus is the water itself.

A truly superb colour combination to rival any spa hotel.

1

2

3

The fabulous colour combination of clean, sleek, modern neutrals shown here will help you to make the most of this area.

Tile the pool area in lead (1), with an edging around the actual pool of marble (4), and paint the unglazed walls in dark stone (2).

4

For around the pool area select loungers and furniture in dark wood similar to woodland brown (3), and add fabric or towels in ink (5).

5

Collector's *character*

Make a real feature of a collection of paintings or photographs.

For something different, choose a selection of differently sized picture frames, but to keep them looking like they belong together use bronze (4) as a finished colour on all of them. Paint the walls in sackcloth. The bronze finish of the frames will lift out of the sackcloth walls.

1

2

3

Keep the flooring in this room bright and light by painting boards or carpeting in ivory (2).

Find odd pieces of wooden furniture in dark oak or walnut (5), keeping the same type of colour or finish but playing with scales and sizes.

4

For your upholstery and curtains, use a combination of stripes, florals and plain cottons in sage (3), sackcloth (1) and ivory. Accessorize with further combinations of these accent colours.

5

Decorating *in Deco*

In many Art Deco images and interiors of the 1920s and 1930s, the main colours are pale, sensual backdrop colours, such as greys, creams, beiges and ivories. Contrasting bolder colours or materials were then employed to give dramatic effect. Why not do the same in your interior?

Deco-inspired schemes for a conservatory or garden room.

1

2

3

Splash out on a beautiful old sandstone (4) or travertine floor. There probably won't be much wall space, but what there is can be painted in sackcloth (1).

Buy contemporary rattan or upholstered chairs and sofas in ivory blush (3), and make simple additional cushions in café au lait (2) and charcoal (5).

4

5

Finally, add contemporary large planters in charcoal and fill with a suitably hardy, slow-growing plant.

Modern *materials*

A design and colour scheme inspired by the iconic Barcelona chair.

The Barcelona chair is renowned for its perfect style, form, comfort and elegance. Mies van der Rohe, the German architect, originally designed the chair for the king and queen of Spain to sit on at the 1929 Barcelona World Exposition.

1

2

3

Execute this scheme in a formal lounge or a large, grand entrance hall or staircase.

At the heart of your chosen room place two Barcelona chairs symmetrically next to each other, in black-brown (3). Sit these on a subtle ivory blush (4) carpet or tiled floor.

4

5

Paint or paper the walls in concrete (1), and find a silk or cotton sateen in copper (5) or milk chocolate (2) to make simple, full-length drapes. Accessorize with large ceramic floor vases, planters or sculptures in black-brown and copper.

Earth *colours*

Before paints were chemically produced, earth colours were used as a paint medium. These earth colours were natural pigments found in their original state in the earth and include red ochres, various shades of yellows and browns and terre vert, a greyish green.

Hues from the earth to create warmth and comfort.

Implement this earthy scheme in a living space – a relaxed and informal zone where you can read, chill out or simply curl up and snooze the afternoon away.

Concrete (1) is a good base grey that can be warmed up by the soft accents of wet clay (2) and pale sand (3). Opt for a natural carpet and simple curtains or blinds in a weighty cotton print of wet clay, pale sand and water (4).

Upholster sofas in natural indigo (5) cotton and add big cotton cushions in pale sand and water. Add bookcases and pictures to complete your retreat.

African *art*

Bold colours and animal prints for an African vision.

One of the hallmarks of Art Deco design was the rich melting pot of cultural influences. The excitement of the African safari, high on the list of "must-sees" for the Art Deco traveller, was recreated in the home through striking items such as a sofa covered in zebra stripe or leopard print, or a primitive tribal-inspired ebony stool.

1

2

3

Why not recreate your own cultural vision? Use clay (1) as your neutral backdrop; paint your walls in this colour and then add simple pale sea green (3) curtains on barely-black (2) poles. Upholster an old chair in animal print, and sit it next to a painted trunk in earth red (5).

4

5

To accessorize, place mustard (4) vases symmetrically next to each other on a shelf or on a piece of furniture, then bring all the bold, earthy tones together in a striped rug.

Taken *from Egypt*

A mystical and regal land that has inspired numerous cultures and movements over time, the ancient Egyptian civilization has it roots in the fertile land around the Nile. Combine the natural colours of the land with the colours of the sky for a bold, fun, yet grown-up scheme that works particularly well in an older child's bedroom.

A scheme inspired by the natural landscape of ancient Egypt.

Paint the main walls in clay (1), then paint one wall or into the alcoves around a chimney breast in Nile blue (3) with peacock (2) on the actual breast.

To adorn the walls, spray wide picture frames in palm (5) and fill with photos, collage boards or abstract prints. Make simple blinds in palm and peacock stripes, and paint cupboards, storage chests or shelving in old-gold (4).

Rolling *landscapes*

Recreate the richness and vitality of the outdoors inside.

The region of Tuscany in central Italy is considered the birthplace of the Renaissance movement and has a rich artistic heritage. This scheme is reminiscent of the lush Italian landscape filled with cypress trees, olive groves and vineyards and soaked in glowing sunshine.

1

2

3

To conjure up the beauty of Tuscany, implement this palette in a lounge or dining room.

Cover the walls in baked clay (1) and add sofas upholstered in rich, velvety olive (4) with the odd statement chair in corn (2).

4

Put in a warm, natural oak floor with a couple of rugs in striped emerald grey (5) and Tuscan yellow (3).

5

Accessorize with cushions and vases or ceramic bowls in any one of these selected colours.

Renaissance *Italy*

An easily translated group of colours, the base of three neutrals is highlighted by pinky reds. Renaissance means "rebirth", or to be born again, and is a word synonymous with change. When giving a room a makeover or a new lease on life you must have a plan or scheme in mind.

Warm neutrals teamed with red and pink accents.

1

2

3

For a bathroom or en suite, choose a rich, warm travertine floor and wall tiles in baked clay (1), and choose a stone mosaic border in a mix of baked clay (1), buttermilk (2) and dark stone (3). This simple application of neutrals will look stunning. Paint any remaining walls in buttermilk.

4

Use garnet (5) as a painted frame for a mirror on the wall or a vase on a window ledge, and finish with a mix of garnet, plaster pink (4) and dark stone towels.

5

Watercolour *wash*

Soft and delicate watercolours for a bedroom.

Watercolours are renowned for their delicacy and translucency. Choose your favourite watercolour painting and you'll find in it a plethora of playful colours. Examine the way they lap over each other, creating new colours and merging softly to form a beautiful series of fluid marks.

1

2

3

In a bedroom, you can be soft and subtle with fabrics and colours and create similar watercolour effects within the room.

Try washing the walls with pastel white (1) and mint (2) for a painterly finish. Drape sheers at the windows in layers of buttermilk (4) that can flap in the wind and diffuse the sunlight. Accent with sunshine tones of peach pink (3) and warm yellow (5). Find your inner artisan and take painterly inspiration by "decorating" a chair or chest of drawers with a simple pattern in peach pink, warm yellow and mint.

4

5

Moody *blues*

Blue is one colour that can be both masculine and feminine, and can work monochromatically. Tranquil blues within a colour scheme lighten the mood, and darker shades can be used for dramatic effect. This undulating range of steel blues will work well in a bright and airy adult room.

Experiment with a range of both deep and light blues.

1

2

3

Paint the walls in pastel white (1). This will help to make the room feel light and airy and thus spacious. Keep all upholstery, curtains and main soft furnishings in blue slate (4).

Accessorize selectively with the remaining ice blue (2), fresh blue (3) and storm blue (5), perhaps by adding a pair of large floor vases in ice blue, for example, or a striped throw in all three. Finally, finish with large, plump cushions of varying textures in storm blue.

4

5

Drawing *from charcoal*

Tones of grey for a serious, sophisticated, contemporary look.

Charcoal is an age-old drawing material. Its flexibility means you can use it to make fine lines and to "tone" or cover large sections of a drawing surface. Playing with tones of colours, such as charcoal, and teaming them with lighter neutrals will help you to create a striking interior.

1

2

3

Colour has an immediate impact on the human eye, and the atmosphere of any room is set by the dominant shades. This scheme would work well in a modern open-plan apartment.

4

5

Choose pieces of furniture in muted basil (4) and black leather (5) to sit in this graphic environment. Pick out accent walls in panther grey (3) that will tone against chalk white (1) as an overall base colour.

Use tones of soft grey (2) for carpet and soft furnishings in a range of textures, and add strong black and white graphic prints and mirrors to finish the look.

Chalky *whites*

Neutrals are key in creating light and airy rooms, and will help you make the most of any light source. All of these selected colours have a similar "strength", so the overall feel will be harmonious and relaxing. These bright, clean colours will work well in a cheery kitchen or sunny bedroom.

Chalky pastels that feel as fresh as a summer's day.

1

2

3

Lime white (2) is the perfect choice for painted furniture and fitted cupboards. Paint the walls in chalk white (1). If it's practical to have a wooden floor, paint it in chalk also, to keep the whole feel of the room fresh and light.

4

Find a pretty floral fabric in sackcloth (5) and light brick (4) that has hints of either lime white or pale peach (3), and use it for upholstery or drapes. To bring contrast into the scheme, use different textures and materials and accessorize with vases or ceramic bowls in any of these beautiful accent colours.

5

Stunning seascapes

Crashing waves, deserted beaches, moody blues and stony greys; nature is our greatest source of inspiration, without us even realizing it. The sea holds a plethora of colours and tones. Pick out varying tones from shells on a beach, sandy neutrals to complement greyish blues and the highlights and low-lights of a stormy sky.

Midnight *blue*

A treasure trove of coastal colour.

Seascapes have always been an inspiration. The clear, shallow coastal waters of the tropical sea are home to an explosion of natural colour combinations, which you can recreate by playing midnight against neon yellow and coral orange.

If you're feeling artistic, paint walls in a child's bedroom or playroom in midnight (1), leaving a blank area or wall on which to create an underwater mural using neon yellow (4), coral orange (5), marine (3) and aqua (2). Paint or carpet the floor in marine and add large, colourful rugs.

Choose bright coral orange for the lamp shades, and paint furniture in aqua and neon yellow for a bright, fun look.

Deep *blue sea*

Blues are known for their calming and soothing properties and are a favourite for bedrooms, bathrooms and studies. However, they can look cold and unwelcoming, so make sure your blue isn't too chilly by choosing one with a warm undertone or by combining it with warm accent colours.

Use the warmth of natural stone to complement blue.

This palette will work well in a sleek, contemporary bathroom.

Use midnight (1) as a wall colour in a bathroom tiled with natural stone in warm heritage cream (4) and grey stone (5). White says "clean" and "fresh", perfect for a bathroom scheme, so add pure white (2) limestone basins and fixtures.

Keep it simple and add towels and accessories in morning mist (3) and midnight.

Stormy *weather*

A steely selection of colours for a classic study.

The range of blue through grey that can be seen in the sea and sky is incomprehensible. Nature offers us a plethora of wondrous colour combinations that are replicated in design over and over, and in a small space dark colours can work well if executed correctly.

Paint walls in storm blue (1) and woodwork in pale grey (2), including any detail, such as fireplace mantels or shelving. Dress the windows in drapes or shades in either pale grey, or pale sea green (5).

Upholster an easy chair in a traditional floral incorporating storm cloud (4) and pale sea green. Add simple cushions in any one of the palette's accent colours and add mirrored and steel blue (3) accessories, such as candlesticks, vases and picture frames, to finish.

Driftwood *art*

There is something deeply romantic about collecting driftwood from the beach and imagining its origins. You can also source ready-made driftwood products that master craftsmen have fashioned into furniture, mirrors and decorative sculptures.

Bleached accent colours to mimic driftwood.

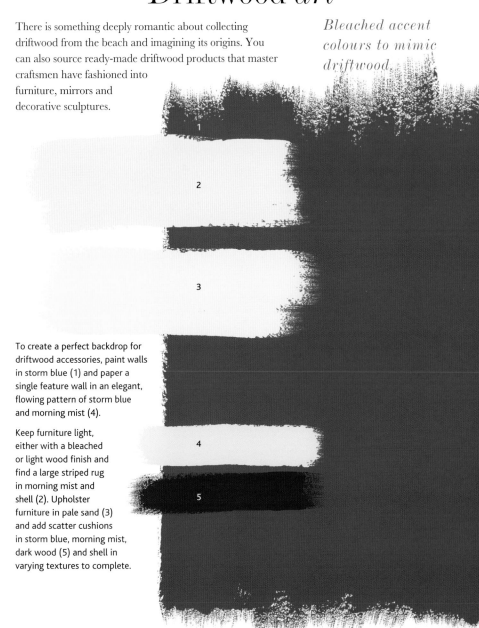

To create a perfect backdrop for driftwood accessories, paint walls in storm blue (1) and paper a single feature wall in an elegant, flowing pattern of storm blue and morning mist (4).

Keep furniture light, either with a bleached or light wood finish and find a large striped rug in morning mist and shell (2). Upholster furniture in pale sand (3) and add scatter cushions in storm blue, morning mist, dark wood (5) and shell in varying textures to complete.

New England *style*

A homely, comfortable scheme that is perfect for family living.

Appliqué cushions, heart details on hand-forged iron hooks, decorative tinplate signs, peg boards, wood-clad walls and shuttered windows all scream New England style. Have fun implementing this scheme in a family living room.

1

2

3

4

5

Incorporate steel (1) into every aspect of the scheme; using it to paint wood shutters could provide the main focus. Paint the walls in blue haze (3), and then decorate them with tin signs and pictures of boats and sea views in wood (5) and steel painted frames.

Cover sofas in a heavy damask fabric in steel and accent with cotton and velvet cushions in baby blue (2) and blue haze. Add simple shaker-style furniture in wood, and upholster a chair or footstool in an American-inspired stripe of red flag (4), steel and white.

Striking *vistas*

The similar-toned colours that make up this palette are yet another way for you to bring the beauty of a seascape into your own home. In order to take full advantage of a great view, maximize windows with simple dressings and use planters inside to draw your eye out to the vista beyond.

Make the most of a beautiful sea view with a pared-down interior.

1

2

3

In a garden room or sunroom, paint what wall area there is in steel (1), and paint all woodwork in pure white (2). In this kind of room the windows are usually the main feature, so take care when dressing them. If you have short windows use simple roller shades in steel, and for larger, tall windows choose a fabric in steel and mocha (3) and use either for curtains or Roman blinds.

4

5

Sum up this scheme with black (4) leather and chrome grey (5) furniture. Lastly, frame the main view with black planters filled with stunning lush green plants.

Rugged *landscape*

Bring the minerals of the earth into a modern bathroom.

When talking of seascapes, it is usually the sea itself that springs to mind, but we mustn't forget the sand, cliffs and jagged rocks that border the coast. Natural stone and marble cut from the earth are simply the most beautiful materials to use in a bathroom.

1

2

3

Base your scheme around a natural marble, and tile the floor and a feature wall in ice (2) and pastel grey (3). Paint the remaining wall space in flint (1).

Add real glamour with a traditional claw-foot tub, and paint the outside and feet in flint.

4

5

Zap colour into this muted theme with zingy textiles. If you have a large window, curtain it in a silk organza in citrine (4) and mid-blue (5), otherwise find a cotton print for a Roman blind. Choose towels and a bath mat in mid-blue to give the room a fresh, modern twist.

Coastal *lines*

The salted air and harsh coastal winds are responsible for the weathered rock and tumbling landscape that make up coastlines. Think of the way the white face of a cliff envelops the sea edge in an elegant, undulating line, and employ this simplicity in an entrance hall.

Seashore simplicity for a light, fresh entrance hall.

1

2

3

Use flint (1) as a paper or paint beneath a chair rail, then paper above it with a classic design in pearl grey (2) and raw silk (3). Keep all woodwork and furniture in the same paint finish of raw silk.

If curtains or blinds are required, stick to a plain silk or voile in mauve (4). If curtains aren't a necessary addition, shade a pair of lamps in mauve instead.

4

5

Finally, add a welcoming, homely touch using cut flowers in traditional cut-glass vases, choosing a contrasting, fresh colour such as pale honey (5).

Côte *d'Azur*

Inspired by the coastal villages of Provence in the south of France.

Transport yourself to the pretty white villages drenched in sunshine, surrounded by lavender fields and overlooking the deep blue sea of the Côte d'Azur coast. Import this beauty by utilizing this scheme in a living or dining room.

1

2

3

4

5

Use Paris blue (1) as the main recurring colour in textiles and upholstery, using a selection of florals, stripes, dots and plain fabrics and as the colour for one accent wall. Paint the remaining walls and floor simply in limestone (2).

Paint a single piece of furniture, such as an old dresser, bookcase or wardrobe, in matte grey (3).

To accent this scheme beautifully use wine (5) as the colour for a pair of accessories, such as lampshades or vases, before adding fresh plants in dark olive (4) and wine.

Mediterranean *breeze*

Give your room a continental twist, taking inspiration from the vibrancy of the terracottas and blues of Mediterranean style. The colour contrasts of this scheme will work exceptionally well in a large family or farmhouse kitchen.

A bold, lively new look for a family kitchen.

1

2

3

Pastel-coloured cabinets create a homely atmosphere, so paint units in Paris blue (1) and sky (2). Contrast these blues with brown mustard (5) walls and rustic wooden worktops in sand (4).

Use a bright, striped fabric that brings the blues and browns together for Roman blinds, and dot authentic Mediterranean kitchen pieces, for example, in wood, earthenware or terracotta, around the room. A rustic wine rack will easily feel at home here too.

4

5

All *calm at sea*

Seductive sea shades for a sumptuous bedroom.

An aquatic palette of bright blues and greens accompanies an eclectic mix of patterns and fabrics. Use this scheme in a master bedroom and transport yourself to a sun-drenched balcony nestled above the water's edge.

1

2

3

4

5

Seduce slate blue (1) walls with an oversized headboard in sea (5), using a sensual fabric – perhaps embroidered or embellished – with plenty of impact. Furnish the room with painted furniture in chalky cream (2), and paint floorboards with driftwood (3).

Choose a luxurious sea kelp (4) and sea (5) bedspread and some decorative cushions in sea kelp. For curtains or blinds keep it simple and either choose wooden Venetian blinds or simple voiles in chalky cream, or use sea for floor-length drapes in a natural silk.

Eastern *promise*

The lotus has its roots in mud and grows upwards through the water, where its petals open out into a beautiful flower. At night the flower closes and disappears underwater, until dawn when it rises and opens again. Featuring extensively in the art of ancient Egypt, it was a symbol of beauty and purity.

A stunning lounge inspired by the colours of the lotus flower.

1

2

3

For a refined and svelte lounge, paint walls in slate blue (1) and carpet the room in haze (2), then use mud (3) for simple Roman blinds and as a main upholstery fabric.

Cover a pair of footstools or small chairs in lotus (4), and cushion the main seating areas using fabrics in a mix of jewel (5), haze, slate blue and lotus.

4

5

Add a pair of ethnic sculptures or vases either side of a fireplace or chimney breast for a hint of Eastern influence.

Windswept *dunes*

Bring the outside in with tones of grass green and sand.

The natural colours of the sea and its surrounding landscape feature prominently in this spring-like scheme. This palette is simple, understated and subtle, using a warm palette of clean colours to freshen the room, and will work well in a light and airy kitchen.

1

2

3

Give a kitchen a fresh look by painting the walls in ice blue (1) and using dune (3) as a base colour for kitchen units and furniture. Brighten up windows with simple roller shades in golden sand (2) that will zing off the ice blue walls.

4

5

Find a chunky oak trestle table with oak benches and add cushioned seat pads upholstered in a mix of rushes (4) and stream green (5). Be creative with your plates and bowls, and bring greens and blues to life in the day-to-day practical accessories you use.

Coastal *retreat*

As reiterated throughout this book, neutrals are great at creating the illusion of a light, airy atmosphere and thus can make the smallest of rooms feel spacious, although sometimes more is needed. In an awkward-shaped entrance or hallway, use this playful selection of colours to make a comfortable space.

Clever colours and ideas to make the most of awkward spaces.

1

2

3

In quirky or old houses you may need to think creatively about how best to use a space. For instance, hallways are often large but not quite large enough to make into a "room" or a defined, usable space.

Make use of walls by creating fixed seating with storage boxes or cupboards underneath painted in rose white (2) and set against a backdrop of ice blue (1). Cover the wooden seats with pretty cushions in brown blush (3), rum butter (5) and midnight (4), mixing florals, stripes, embroidered and plain fabrics.

4

5

Boats *in harbour*

A bright, exciting and fun scheme for a boy's room.

Little boys love boats, and this nautical scheme is perfect for a boy's bedroom or playroom. Working in horizontal stripes, paint the top 65 percent of the walls in dusky blue, then, working down, paint the next 20 percent in royal blue and the remaining 15 percent in meadow green (4).

1

2

3

To implement a true nautical style, mix wood and pure white (3) painted furniture throughout the room.

Find fun items to put into the room that are in keeping with the style, such as boat-shaped shelving, a traditional hammock and large model boats.

4

5

Paint the floor in pure white and add funky rugs in dusky blue (1) and seaweed (5). Bed linen can adopt any one or a combination of these colours. To finish, put royal blue (2) shades at the windows with pure white voile drapes.

Weathered *beach huts*

These pastel, bleached colours are not just for sweet, pretty girls' rooms. If used correctly and in a contemporary way, they can have real impact and will create a stunning bedroom for anyone or alternatively, a beautiful lounge.

A pretty blend of perfect pastels to brighten any room.

1

2

3

Hang long granite gray (5) drapes in a heavy woven cotton or velvet at the windows, against the subtle wall colour of dusky blue (1). For upholstery, use a combination of silver-cream (2) and bunting pink (3), keeping it neat and unfussy so these pastels don't look too sickly.

4

5

Carpet in silver-cream and powder blue (4), or choose a woven rug if you have floorboards.

Add a striking standard lamp with a dark wood base and a silver-cream shade to sit against the dusky blue walls, and find room for a large powder blue vase or glass ornament.

Colourful *vintage*

An explosion of 1950s vacation colour.

Grab a mai tai and go tropical with a scheme that radiates happiness and enjoyment. The bright, cheerful accents of this palette work exceptionally well with tranquil pale ocean and used cleverly will bring your chosen room to life, without overdoing it.

Pale ocean (1) is a beautiful, crisp, fresh backdrop for these heady pinks and blues. Ground the intense colour with wet sand (4), used for flooring in the form of shaggy rugs or carpet, and choose low-level furniture in kitsch patterns in a mix of Hawaiian blue (2), marine (3) and wet sand.

Add beanbags, small upholstered stools or floor cushions in prints and plains in marine and paradise pink (5). Finally, dig out retro lamps, unusual period prints and other 1950s pieces to really bring the scheme together.

Deserted *beach*

An atmospheric bedroom scheme that evokes images of the sun setting over the sea on a winter afternoon. Combining the fresh, light neutrals of the beach with the deepest blue of the ocean and the rich brown of African walnut will help you capture the essence of coastal living, wherever you may live.

A natural palette for your very own beach paradise.

1

2

3

To create a beachy retreat in your home, collect natural objects, interesting shells, stones, driftwood and old crates for effortless chic.

Contrast African walnut (5) furniture against pale ocean (1) walls. Find nautical fabrics, such as stripes and natural linens, in shell (2), cloud (3) and ink (4), and use them to make cushion covers with ties and loose covers for chairs. Give everything a "crafty" edge to complete the concept.

4

5

Classic flora

A collection of schemes influenced by the beauty
of flowers. Take inspiration from the colours and
tones found naturally in some of nature's sweetest
flora: violets, lavenders, irises and wisteria. Violets
are creative and have expressive tones that are
sensual, stimulating and emotional. Close your
eyes and imagine the soft, silky texture of a petal,
and interpret this delicate image in your colour
scheme and the fabrics you use.

Beauty *of the Amazon*

Degrees of blue-violet create a moody, rich bedroom hideaway.

An undulating green carpet of vegetation punctuated by areas of water, the Amazon is one of the most diverse and unexplored natural environments on the planet. This colour scheme takes its inspiration from the mystery of this wondrous area.

1

2

3

4

5

Be bold with deep, exotic blackberry (1) on the walls, punctuated by a cloud (2) chair rail and cornice in a matte finish, so the look doesn't become brash. Upholster an oversized headboard in cloud, in a shiny fabric such as velvet or silk.

For a dazzling explosion of colour, curtain in violet (4), letting the sheer weight of the colour shine through, rather than using a fussy heading or design. Upholster a chair in Amazon blue (5), choosing a shiny fabric to give the chair impact against the dark walls. Add grey (3) accessories for a sleek finish.

Lakeside *retreat*

This scheme conjures up an image of a log cabin tucked away in a forest and overlooking a moody black lake. A deep, dark scheme such as this is perfect for a dining room that is used predominantly in the evening, and it provides lots of scope for the addition of brighter accents.

A beautiful selection of woodland colours to dine among.

Paint the focal wall – one that is free of features such as windows or doors – in twilight (5) and the others in blackberry. To adorn, add artwork to the focal wall in blackberry (1) and gooseberry (3).

Upholster dining chairs in glorious rich moss (4) edged with fern green (2), and follow these greens through to accessories, such as table runners, glassware and candlesticks. Twilight is also a great colour to accessorize the room with, and combining it with the other natural hues in this palette will result in a stunning overall look.

Winter *pansies*

Zest up a dark space with the colours of cheery winter pansies.

The pansy is an often overlooked plant, but its petals of white, pink, blue or violet sparkle even on the most overcast of days and can bring pleasure and colour to the dull winter months. Take inspiration from these flowers and use them to enliven a dark, dull, tired or small space.

1

2

3

Bring some bold sunshine colours into a child's playroom by painting alternating walls in crocus (4) and hot orange (5). This will lift fantastically off a rich deep violet (1) rubber floor, which is not only soft underfoot but durable and practical as well.

4

Into one of the corners of the room suspend a hammock in deep violet, pale violet (3) and lemon cream (2) or a funky plastic hanging chair.

5

To complete, accessorize with round rugs in crocus and hot orange and furniture painted in lemon cream.

Bluebell *woods*

Spring is a season associated with life and new beginnings, and there is no clearer sign that spring is here than a forest floor carpeted in bluebells. The mass of deep blue-violet lapping at the edges of green grass and punctuated by the dark bark of tree trunks translates into a stunning room scheme.

A spring palette to transform any study.

Paint the walls in deep violet (1) and carpet the room in grey bark (3). Add a Victorian desk in a warm oak or mahogany finish and an old chair upholstered in foliage green (4) leather.

For blinds and curtains, keep the look studious and sophisticated; choose a masculine fabric, such as a simple weave or check in grey bark and lavender blue (5).

Finally, make a centrepiece of a striking piece of glass or a large ceramic sculpture in gorgeous bluebell (2).

Nature's *renaissance*

An unusual group of colours with a fresh, contemporary edge.

Although bright and modern, these colours are all drawn from nature. This scheme is perfect for a beach house or cottage on the coast and is sure to promote calm and relaxation wherever you choose to implement it.

1

2

3

Use pure white (2) as a painted floor, and paint walls in regal blue (1); you may want to add random stripes or stars in pure white (2).

Add deep, comfy sofas in regal blue denim cotton and antique pieces of chunky, deep earth brown (5) furniture, which will work perfectly with the blue and white hues.

4

5

Tease the regal theme by accessorizing with cushions, throws, and trinkets in pink peach (3) and hot pink (4).

The *herb garden*

Fresh herbs not only taste fantastic and smell amazing, they also show a diverse range of colours and textures, which are the inspiration behind this group of colours.

Bring the lush richness of the garden into the bedroom.

1

2

3

Regal blue (1), like the leaves of blue basil, can be used as a main colour for a truly organic bedroom. Offset the blue with gentle thyme flower (2) as an upholstered headboard and carpet or painted floor.

4

5

Frame windows with full drapes of purple sage (4), and add decadent tassels or tiebacks made from crystals in thyme flower. Pile the bed high with cushions in minted blue (5) edged with mustard yellow (3) and purple sage.

Fresh, *bright and lifting*

The mix of cool and warm tones here gives an unexpected edge.

Sometimes you need to be bold in your design choices. If you are ready for a change, try this energizing palette. It would work particularly well in an open-plan living or work space—perhaps a studio or warehouse apartment.

1

2

3

Paint most of the walls in deep blueberry (1), but pick out a few in grey light (2). Use deep blueberry for large, key items in the room, for example as high-gloss kitchen units, with a worktop in grey light and contrasting aqua white (3) bar stools.

4

5

Use a bright rug in citrus tones (4, 5) to define the living or working area of the space, and add dark sofas in deep blueberry.

To finish, pick out individual items in bright colours, for example, a footstool in aqua white or a floor vase in citrus orange (4).

Pretty *pastels*

Pastels don't have to be boring or reserved merely for girls' bedrooms, just make sure you use them in the right finish and application. These colours sit best with natural fabrics and woods, not shiny metal or perfect finishes.

Choose soft pastels for a cozy, private hideaway.

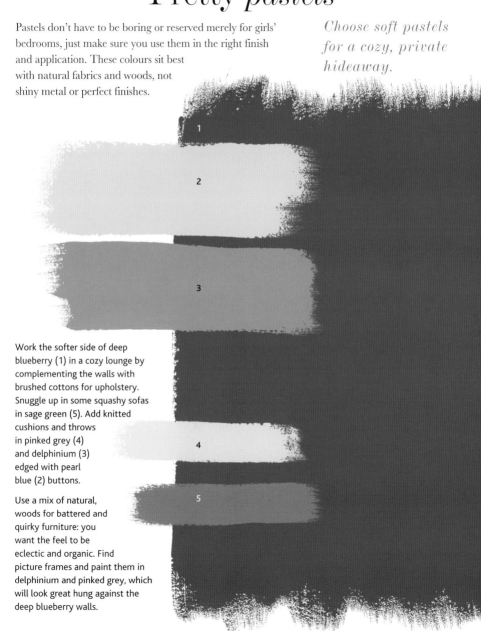

Work the softer side of deep blueberry (1) in a cozy lounge by complementing the walls with brushed cottons for upholstery. Snuggle up in some squashy sofas in sage green (5). Add knitted cushions and throws in pinked grey (4) and delphinium (3) edged with pearl blue (2) buttons.

Use a mix of natural, woods for battered and quirky furniture: you want the feel to be eclectic and organic. Find picture frames and paint them in delphinium and pinked grey, which will look great hung against the deep blueberry walls.

Hunting *for truffles*

The velvety grey-brown of truffles sits perfectly with violets.

The most expensive edible fungi, truffles are found around the bases of oak and chestnut trees in the forests of France and Italy. They are revered for their taste and supposed aphrodisiac properties, and their colour is the inspiration for this scheme.

1

2

3

In a large drawing or sitting room, paint the main walls in iris (1). If the room has a wooden fireplace mantel, paint it natural stone (3), a colour that sits beautifully against iris. If the fireplace needs replacing or creating, commission a simple design in real stone.

4

5

Carpet the floor in rich, velvety truffle (2), choosing a soft, deep-pile carpet that looks sumptuous and feels fabulous underfoot. Add upholstered furniture in a mix of lichen (4) and granite blue (5), and accessorize in iris and truffle.

Violet *surprise*

The word "violet" is commonly associated with the flower from which the name is derived. These flowers are a shade of purple that is a mixture of both blue and red and are the colour basis for this palette. This violet scheme could be applied anywhere but works especially well in a kitchen.

Beautiful violets that translate well in a kitchen.

1

2

3

Use iris (1) as the main colour for walls and play off this colour with kitchen units painted in a mixture of violet white (2) and dark stone (3), using more of one colour than the other so that the units don't look too even.
Use indigo (5) as a worktop color for the full run of the kitchen.

4

Finish with vibrant blue-violet (4) kitchen stools or chairs, which look funky and fun, and accessorize with cookware in either violet white or dark stone and beautiful dinnerware in any of these colours, or a combination of all of them.

5

By *the stream*

Where better to replicate water than the bathroom?

Water has many distinct properties. It is integral to the world and the proliferation of its life-forms. It has various religious symbolisms and is explored in many arts. Embracing the calming and reflective qualities of water in interiors is an important aspect of the ancient art of feng shui.

1

2

3

Simply by replicating the colours of water you can bring its calming, soothing benefits into your own environment.

Paint bluebell (1) on the walls and any tongue-and-groove panelling that you may have. Find a beautiful natural stone or travertine floor tile in blush stone (4) and clay (5); alternatively, paint floorboards in blush stone.

4

5

To finish the scheme, add towels and accessories in metallic blue (2) and Amazon blue (3).

Summer *fields*

Imagine yourself on a bright and sunny Sunday afternoon, meandering through the fields and absorbing the heady aromas of summertime. To bring the memories of this perfect time into your home, try implementing this scheme in your living room or a more formal lounge.

A selection of summertime colours perfect for a lounge.

1

2

3

Paint or paper walls in bluebell (1), and paint the inside fascia of a fireplace or a dresser or large piece of furniture in powder blue (4). Upholster sofas in apple white (2) and lake (5), using a striped fabric or one with a subtle pattern encompassing these two colours.

4

Dress windows in simple curtains in corn (3) edged along the bottom in lake if you wish. Pull all of these gentle colours together with accessories, cushions and objects d'art.

5

In *bloom*

A fresh, fragrant, floral delight to adorn a living room.

Both the colour and beauty of flowers have always been an inspiration to artists and designers alike. The essence of flowers – their shape, texture and colour – have been depicted throughout centuries, but it is difficult to capture their freshness and scent.

1

2

3

4

5

Capture these floral qualities by employing these colours in a domestic setting. Delicate cornflower (1) is a cool blue with grey undertones, suited to a lounge or living room.

A warm, natural oak floor would work well against cornflower walls. Alternatively, use natural burlap (3) as a carpet or floor covering. Use lily pink (2) for traditional upholstery, mixed with antique leather (5) for the odd chair or footstool.

Add curtains or blinds in heavy woven fabrics in deep cornflower (4) and natural burlap.

Earth *tones*

This book features a number of schemes that draw upon nature and the world around us, and this group of colours is another that does so. For a relaxed and amiable scheme, tone these warm, earthy neutrals with the cooler, contrasting, limestone-like qualities of cornflower.

A scheme that reflects the natural earth around us.

1

2

3

4

5

Implement this scheme in an entrance hall for a stunning, contemporary look. Carpet the floor and the stairs in a cornflower (1) runner. Paint the staircase and above the dado rail in light sand (2), and use cornflower below it – this looks particularly striking if the walls are panelled.

Upholster window seats or occasional chairs in light tan (4) or soft, earth brown (5) leather. Complete the look with a selection of fabrics and accessories in khaki (3), cornflower and light sand.

Secret *garden*

Fall in love instantly with this dreamy bouquet of colours.

Flowers provide enjoyment for many, whether in the neat colourful beds of the garden, growing wild in fields or meadows or carefully arranged in vases. Like the heady scent of freshly picked flowers, these gorgeous floral-inspired colours will work well in a bedroom.

1

2

3

Paint or paper the walls in hyacinth (1) and carpet in the same hue, giving the room a dreamlike quality, all fluffy and feminine. If you want to include a feature wall, look for hyacinth wallpaper with hints of green stone (2) and darker bark green (5).

4

5

Go ultra girly and curtain in rose (3) and hyacinth in a delicate floral fabric, or go more neutral with bark green (5) and gooseberry (4). Upholstery should tie in with the choice of curtaining, but if you have chosen a fussy curtain fabric, use a simple single shade for upholstery, and vice versa.

Sweet *dreams*

Continuing with the soft, fragrant, delicate qualities of flowers, consider the silky-soft texture of a rose petal, how sensual it is to touch, and try to recreate that feel with tactile fabrics. The softness and femininity of this scheme makes it ideal for a girly bedroom.

A floral scheme perfect for a little girl's bedroom.

1

2

3

Paint the walls in hyacinth (1), reserving one wall or a chimney breast for a simple mural of hearts or dots and stars in lilac (2), rich cream (3) and hyacinth – you could even embellish the mural with stick-on crystals and buttons.

4

Carpet the room in fudge (4) or, as a lighter alternative, paint floorboards in rich cream.

5

Paint furniture in rich cream, with fun coloured handles in lilac. Choose simple cotton bedding in latte (5) and fudge (4), with pretty dress pillows in lilac and hyacinth.

Changing *seasons*

A palette driven by the changing colours of autumn.

As leaves change colour through the year, trees and foliage can offer an infinite number of colour permutations and combinations to draw upon. Combine the warmth of autumn colours with cooler grey tones for a beautiful lounge.

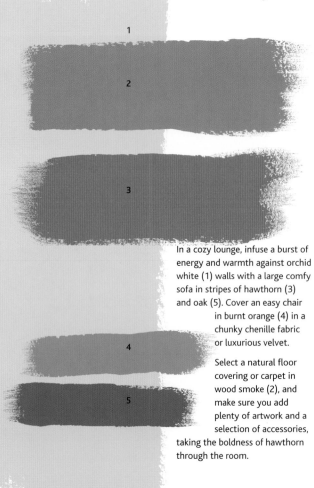

1

2

3

In a cozy lounge, infuse a burst of energy and warmth against orchid white (1) walls with a large comfy sofa in stripes of hawthorn (3) and oak (5). Cover an easy chair in burnt orange (4) in a chunky chenille fabric or luxurious velvet.

4

5

Select a natural floor covering or carpet in wood smoke (2), and make sure you add plenty of artwork and a selection of accessories, taking the boldness of hawthorn through the room.

Grand, *elegant Victorian charm*

Victorian colours are generally thought of as dark, muted tones, but they do work wonderfully well in large, formal settings. Team neutrals with deep, rich accents for a traditional feel and to inject a sense of grandeur into a formal lounge, dining or drawing room.

Rich, classic colours for traditional splendour.

1

2

3

Paint walls in Regency green (2), punctuating this deep, classical colour with a dado rail, picture rail, cornice and all woodwork finished in orchid white (1).

Contrast orchid white floorboards with deep, rich walnut (5) furniture. Upholster dining chair seat pads or full chairs or sofas in gorgeous biscuit (4) velvet.

4

5

Place tall glass lamps with huge silk shades in rose peach (3) on a sideboard or console table to finish.

Return to nature

Immerse yourself in healing green. Calming, energizing and stimulating, greens are an ideal way to bring the outside into our homes. This chapter focuses on those colours found naturally in the landscapes around us. Simply look outside your window. Be inspired and ignited by what surrounds you; falling leaves of autumnal neutrals against hints of silver birch, secret clearings deep in the forest, placid lakes and still skies.

Lush *mangroves*

Blend the garden room and garden.

The colours of nature are an amazing source of inspiration from which we should take reference. In this palette, green – the colour of life and growth – is the primary focus, and will help you bring the freshness of the outside in. Use this scheme to extend the outdoors into a conservatory or summer house.

Paint the walls within the conservatory or summer house in tranquil buff (3), and mirror this outside by painting an external wall in the same colour.

Reflect the greens in the vegetation outside by using seaweed (1) for conservatory furniture, with shades of foliage (4) and green earth (5) in loose cushions.

Finally, take praline (2) wood flooring through the conservatory and outside to a decked patio to create the perfect environment for a glass of wine with friends.

Summer *meadows*

When an area of grassland is left uncultivated, the very ordinary but beautiful flowers and plants that punctuate the expanse of green are simply breathtaking. Irregular patterns, varying colours and heavenly scents all make for perfect inspiration.

Create an eclectic mix of meadow colours for a traditional bedroom.

To recreate this summer mix in a bedroom, paint a seaweed (1) feature wall behind a traditional wrought-iron bed. Paint some shaker-style bedside tables in alpine white (2), and use the same colour on the remaining walls for a striking contrast to the dark seaweed.

Buy colourful patchwork quilts and comforters in mulberry (5), dusky mauve (4) and grass (3), and a selection of plain cushions covered in any one of these accent colours. To finish, place pretty vases of wildflowers on the bedside table.

Nature's *finery*

For a formal dining room keep things ordered and symmetrical.

This palette makes use of the hues of nature's woodland. The deep greens and rich browns shown here are ideal for a formal setting – either a dining or formal reception room. To make an impression, you need good-quality furniture and fabrics, as well as a refined approach to decoration.

Lighting is an essential part of a good dining experience: you don't want to be blinded, but at the same time you would like to see what you are eating.

Paint the walls in rich sage green (1) and add pairs of contemporary wall lights with conker (3) wood bases and yellow-cream (4) shades. Keep furniture to a minimum, just a large table and a sideboard in conker-colored (3) wood, and upholster chairs in simple but elegant warm stone (5). Curtain with floor-length drapes in putty (2).

Unexplored *landscape*

It is relatively easy to decorate large rooms. In smaller spaces, you need to think carefully about colours and maximizing space. Choose quiet greys and blue-greens for a snug or home office, remembering that in small spaces it's important to keep clutter hidden and ensure that what is on display is attractive and neat.

In small spaces work up schemes with gentle hues.

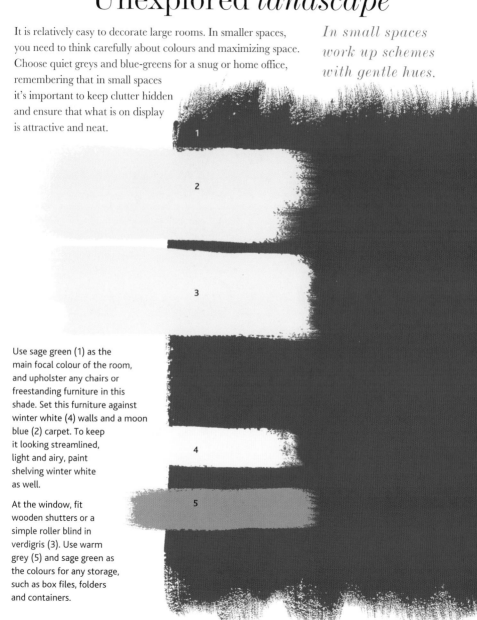

Use sage green (1) as the main focal colour of the room, and upholster any chairs or freestanding furniture in this shade. Set this furniture against winter white (4) walls and a moon blue (2) carpet. To keep it looking streamlined, light and airy, paint shelving winter white as well.

At the window, fit wooden shutters or a simple roller blind in verdigris (3). Use warm grey (5) and sage green as the colours for any storage, such as box files, folders and containers.

Silver *birch*

Cool, sophisticated colours for a classic drawing room.

Using a cool, calm and collected palette, lift ash grey perfectly by adding icy blue and dove grey, before combining these with further green accents. These timeless colours are suited to both period and contemporary settings.

1

2

3

This scheme can work in any kind of room if used thoughtfully. For a dramatic effect use ash grey (1) and meadow green (5) as your main wall colours. For a more subtle scheme, use barely there icy blue (2) and dove grey (3). Dove grey (3) will also make a fabulous carpet or floor colour in this scheme.

4

5

Re-cover an old chair or sofa in deep moss (4) velvet for a rich, luxurious finish. Use the remaining colours for cushions, curtains and other accents.

Sun-drenched *orchard*

Imagine the sun soaking an apple orchard or flooding a citrus grove or a large, woven basket filled with the ripened fruits collected from this forest garden. This palette takes reference from this rural scene and is the perfect kitchen scheme for a rambling farmhouse or converted barn.

A fresh, fruity scheme inspired by rural living.

1

2

3

For the centrepiece of a family country kitchen, nothing beats a gorgeous vintage stove; choose pale apple (2) if you can.

Paint the walls of your chosen room with ash grey (1), and find some beautiful backsplash tiles in shades of ash grey and mint white (3).

4

Mix kitchen units in warm oak with golden (4) and straw (5) hand-painted cupboards for a rustic, country look. Accessorize with similar rustic-style cookware.

5

Shimmering *light*

Unusual dark colours paired with flashes of bright highlights.

The effect of light upon water is the main inspiration for this dramatic palette. Freshen-up a canal green base with a combination of both light and dark accents for a lavish vintage bedroom in true 1930s-style glamour.

1

2

3

Use classic glass table lamps and geometric mirrors to throw light around canal green (1) walls. Upholster an oversized headboard in raspberry (4) silk, buttoned and edged with bitter chocolate (5), and add wall lights either side of the bed in bitter chocolate.

4

Place a chaise longue under a window, upholstered in a devoré print of raspberry and acorn (3), with bitter chocolate feet.

5

Carpet the room in ivory (2) to balance the dark colours, and accessorize with Deco sculptures.

Evoking *twilight*

The unusual ambient light of twilight has long been popular with painters and photographers, who refer to it as the "blue hour", after the French expression *l'heure bleue*. As night draws in, these twilight colours will create an escape from the traumas of the working day.

Mysterious and soothing muted colours evoke a calming ambience.

Use dusk sky (2) as an evocative neutral for a feature wall; its hints of grey and pink make for a mysterious tone. Bring canal green (1) in for the remaining walls, and curtain in a lighter shade of this colour with hints of deep teal (4).

Stain a wooden floor in rich nutmeg (3); all the better if the wood is a little battered and not too perfect.

Upholster elegant and comfortable sofas in canal green, and fluff up with extra cushions in spearmint (5) and deep teal. Light the fire and numerous candles and begin to unwind.

Natural *stone*

Warm tonal greens and creams ideal for a child's bedroom.

Wild and garish colours are not always desired for a child's room – it can be far more restful to create an inviting, calming space. However, children's rooms should be interesting and fun, with plenty of storage and decoration to inspire.

1

2

3

Use warm stone (1) as your wall colour and sand (2) as the hue for a hard-wearing but soft carpet. Into an alcove add painted shelves in pale yellow (3).

Fill the shelves with books, and glue rows of shells, chestnuts and acorns in box frames to create natural artworks that look stylish and smart.

4

5

Use pale yellow for bedroom furniture with foliage (4) handles, and add a fun striped or checked rug in lake (5) and pale yellow to complete this stylish child's bedroom.

Past *antiquities*

If you have collected pieces of furniture or artefacts from travels, it's always nice to be able to display them but in a relaxed way; you don't want to feel like you're living in a museum! The trick is to group items of similar colour or type and keep the decor in the room pared down and neutral.

A scheme that will evolve beautifully over time.

1

2

3

Warm stone (1) is a great warm neutral that can be used as a backdrop in any room. Use this shade to cover your walls.

Rose lip (2) is an unusual tone but gives a fresh look for upholstery fabric on old wing chairs. It also works especially well with muted orange (3), a classic colour for drapes.

4

5

Use warm stone, avocado (4) and blackish-green (5) as colours for further upholstery. Finish with accessories in any of these colours or a combination of all of them.

Autumnal *richness*

Bring the rich, warm colours of autumn into a dining room.

The ochres and varying browns of autumn leaves are the inspiration behind this palette. These seasonal, rich tones are perfect for a warm and homely dining room scheme but will also work equally well in a cozy lounge or living area.

1

2

3

4

5

For your base, paint the walls of your chosen room in natural limestone (1), and make a feature of the wall opposite the main window by painting it poppy (5).

Place a console table in cocoa bean (3) against the poppy wall, and add a pair of lamps with cinnamon (2) shades. Mirror this on the dining table with a finish in cocoa bean, and a table runner that combines khaki green (4) and cinnamon.

Upholster chairs in cinnamon to complete the ensemble.

Crisp, *fresh and inviting*

Snow-covered landscapes, steely winter skies and snowdrops peeking through the spring ground; be inspired by the cool, calming time of year when hope is restored and we look forward to the warmth of summer.

Crisp, relaxed colours for an entrance that welcomes visitors.

1

2

3

Tile the floor that leads off into a kitchen or dining room in natural limestone (1).

Panel the hall and paint the panelling in limestone also, so it seamlessly flows from one application to another. Paint the wall above in misted pink (2).

4

Add a pair of ceramic umbrella stands or decorative floor vases in icicle (3), pinked taupe (4) or apple cream (5) to frame the start of the hall and make for an inviting finish.

5

Woodland *fell*

Use the subtle shades of nature in a bedroom.

You might come upon these shades on a nature ramble, but their quiet beauty is equally at home in a modern apartment. A resourceful colour, brown stone mixed with the calming shade of marble is ideal for sleeping spaces.

In a bedroom, use marble (1) as the main wall colour with brown stone (2) painted bedside tables and furniture. Khaki green (3), petal (4) or tobacco (5) would make a fabulous headboard in a textured linen fabric or raw silk and look great against fresh bed linen in petal. Adorn the bed with plump cushions in the same shade chosen for the headboard.

This scheme also works well in a modern open-plan kitchen/living space. In a kitchen, try the work surfaces in tobacco, and paint units in petal and brown stone (2).

Misty *morning*

This scheme was inspired by a brisk stroll in the early morning. As the sunlight begins to burn through the mist, the landscape becomes clear and refined. Implement this light, fresh scheme in an interior for a graceful, elegant living space.

Layer warm and cool neutrals for a stylish living room.

Utilizing a scheme that layers both warm and cool neutrals in a room will help you transcend light and dark. Use ambiguous marble (1) as a cheery base neutral for your living area, and couple with the darkest accent in the group – flagstone grey (3) – as flooring. Add contemporary sofas upholstered in taupe (2) leather, and place large floor cushions in bluebell grey (5) around a central coffee table.

Use rain cloud (4) to create your own full-length drapes that hang simply and make a feature of the windows, and accessorize with any of these accent shades.

Bracken, *moss and ferns*

Promote relaxation with a range of leafy tones.

Green is synonymous with nature and energy. It's calming, restful and balanced, so anywhere you want to relax will benefit from an injection of this colour. If you have a large bathroom make the most of these relaxing tones to create a perfect hideaway.

1

2

3

Use bath stone (1) as the colour for both wall and floor tiles. Paint any remaining wall space in foliage (2), and use deep forest (5) and the other green tones for plump towels and bathroom accessories.

4

Paint the exterior of a claw-foot tub in soft wood (3), and keep the fixtures in clean, fresh pure white (4).

5

A natural oak would also work with these tones, so if you have space for freestanding furniture you may consider bringing in this finish.

Lost *in the forest*

Enter a forest and you begin a magical journey through whispering trees and unknown territories—a feeling that you can replicate at home. Find a beautiful, subtle floral-inspired wallpaper that brings together bath stone and pebble grey, and use it to paper the whole room or just one wall.

Replicate the mysteries of a deep, tree-lined forest in a bedroom.

1

2

3

With your walls ready, carpet the room or paint floorboards in warm bath stone (1). Pick a plain woven fabric in field green (3) for window dressings; Roman blinds in this shade edged with pebble grey (4) and with natural leather pulls will look fabulous.

4

5

Choose a contemporary deep serpentine (5) four-poster bed with simple lines as a focal point of the room. At the foot of the bed, upholster a footstool or bench in vibrant jade (2) for a flash of strong colour.

Beauty
of the desert

Warming and enlivening, the sunshine tones of yellows
will inject soul into any interior space. From pared-
down yellow-creams to pigment-rich golden saffrons,
use yellows as a base to brighten and lighten cooler
north-facing spaces. Take inspiration from the midday
heat of the Kalahari Desert – its space and clay-baked
landscape. Imagine dried-out grasses strewn across an
expanse of golden sand and the hot sun scorching the
earth beneath, and implement the warmth of browns,
yellows and oranges at home.

Lost *oasis*

A bright, fun and energizing scheme fit for a bedroom.

Reminiscent of the hot, dry desert, the warm ochres of this palette work especially well with contrasting cool accents. While the almost tropical tones are lively and energizing, the cool blue components of the group will give a calmer edge to the scheme, perfect for an older child's bedroom or study.

1

2

3

In your chosen room, paint walls in bright sunflower (1) for a bright, bold backdrop.

Choose the lightest colour, desert cream (4), as a carpet or painted floor. If you decide to paint the floor, add funky rugs in pool (2), azure (3), sunflower and rich golden (5).

4

5

For curtains, choose a stylized floral or patterned print that brings all of these colours together, and frame pop-art-style prints in white box frames and hang them in sets on the walls to finish the look.

Bazaar *style*

Imagine the old bazaar in Cairo; busy, bustling, noisy streets lined with colourful stalls selling cloth, clothing, spices, foodstuffs, traditional jewellery and souvenirs. For understated elegance take inspiration from the tactile qualities of these items, particularly the fabrics.

Take inspiration from the colours of an Egyptian bazaar.

1

2

3

Be adventurous and upholster a modern L-shaped sofa in bright sunflower (1). Against a neutral backdrop of natural (2) and grey sand (3), a velvet, chenille or leather sofa in this shade will look like a real designer statement.

4

Accentuate the boldness of the sofa choice with beautiful cushions in cooler blackcurrant (4) and golden brown (5), using patterns and embroidered pieces as well as plains. To complete the look, add authentic pieces in any of these colours.

5

Nomadic *charm*

Unique and luxurious, combine unusual colours with dark woods.

This scheme has only two basic colours, but by playing with the shades and their applications you can ensure the room feels rich and luxurious. Combine this palette with dark wood, mirrored finishes and good quality furniture for a deluxe and stunning overall effect.

1

2

3

The centrepiece of the room could be a huge yellow-ochre (1) drum-pendant light shade, which will look amazing against matte dusky mauve (3) walls.

Use a sumptuous eggplant (5) velvet for the sofa and yellow ochre and India yellow (4) silk for cushions to really intensify the injection of yellow in the scheme.

4

5

Find a textured, silky large rug in mushroom (2) for the centre of the room, and finish with ornate mirrors and gilt frames on the walls.

Scorched *earth*

Light, bright or cool colours are the stereotypical colours for a bathroom – cool blues, greys or whites, for example – and so you might not think this is a suitable palette for such a room. But if you have a reasonably sized room and the space to accommodate a freestanding tub it's perfect.

A warm but relaxed and gentle scheme fit for a bathroom.

1

2

3

Paint the walls in yellow ochre (1) and the external face of the tub in dark stone (3).

Use burlap (2) as a floor colour and find colonial pieces of freestanding furniture and accessories in dark wood to contrast with the floor.

4

For the window, make a simple shade in yellow ochre edged with dark stone, and use mirrors to maximize the light.

5

Finally, choose a selection of plain and striped towels in pot pink (4), terracotta (5) and burlap.

Spice *market*

An opulent set of spicy colours, perfect for a dining room.

The spice trade developed in the Middle East in around 2000 BCE, and in the Middle Ages spices were among the most luxurious products available in Europe. Their aromatic flavourings are the inspiration for these rich tones, which combine to create a chic, elegant scheme.

1

2

3

4

5

Find antique furniture in rich mahogany (2) and reupholster the chairs in golden saffron (1). Replicate golden saffron, but not necessarily in the same fabric, in full-length curtains to enhance the ceiling height. Paint the walls in elephant (4); the yellow tones of saffron look fabulous next to matte grey paint.

Lighting is crucial to setting the right ambiance in a dining room, so pair lamps on a sideboard or console table with oversized shades in jet (5), and in a corner place a standard lamp with a similarly shaped shade in burlap (3).

Windswept *dunes*

Picture an open expanse of golden sand dunes, unspoiled and seemingly endless, falling softly against the surrounding coastal landscape from which the dunes are forged. Use these colours to create your very own indoor paradise, an ideal respite from the demands of daily life.

Warm a pastel scheme with soft textures and dark wood.

1

2

3

In a lounge, choose a dramatic wallpaper in golden saffron (1) and lily (2) to act as a backdrop to grey-lilac (3) upholstered furniture. Add woven throws and woollen cushions in grey-lilac, gold tint (4) and clay (5).

4

Carpet the sitting area in clay (5), or, if you have a wood floor, use a large textured rug to define a cozy area.

5

To complete, find a complementary fabric that brings lily and grey-lilac tones (2, 3) and golden saffron together, and hang simple curtains from a luxurious, chunky dark-wood pole.

Mexican *hot*

A sizzling scheme ideal for a modern living space.

Fiery, hot and spicy, the Mexican influence in this scheme is energizing, outgoing and above all, fun. Mix orange and brown with the warm tones of buttermilk for a scheme that would work well in a modern lounge or open-plan living area.

1

2

3

Paint two adjoining walls in rich buttermilk (1) and the rest with an inoffensive neutral such as beige linen (3), which will allow the yellow to be the star and lead the eye into the area you've chosen to define.

4

5

Use pure white (2) for the woodwork. Find a good retro fabric for window blinds in rich buttermilk and hot orange (4).

Pick out key accessories in hot orange, perhaps a funky chair in the corner or a fabulous lamp, and finish with dark wood (5) contemporary furniture in simple, clean shapes.

Pared-down *living*

Cheery, bright and refreshing, yellow is the colour associated with sunshine and light. Yellow works particularly well with greens and oranges and can be either brightened or subdued, depending on the accents it is teamed with. Seen as welcoming and upbeat, it is perfect for a kitchen or hallway.

Use yellow to bring a little sunshine into the room.

1

2

3

What better place to employ the attributes of rich buttermilk (1) than on the walls of an entrance hall, where you welcome guests into your home?

Keep the woodwork in clean white (3), which works extremely well with all yellows. Choose a woven runner in sage (2), yellowed cream (4), and gold ochre (5), remembering that stripes are particularly smart for hall and stair runners.

4

5

Add some greenery in gold ochre and yellowed cream pots on the window ledges or furniture tops to complete the look.

Californian *cactus*

For a modern palette opt for zesty yellows and lime greens.

This scheme combines the warm, arid colour of sandstone with fragrant citrus accents. The subtlety of warm sandstone is complemented perfectly by these sharp, refreshing shades, resulting in a bold scheme, ideal for a contemporary kitchen.

1

2

3

Warm sandstone (1) has delicate cream-yellow tones that make it ideal for a painted kitchen, but keep the overall feeling light with worktops, handles and tiling in cream (3).

4

For a bright, refreshing wake-up call, include flashes of colour in lime green (5).

5

Paint an old kitchen table in honey (2), leaving the top in wood or painted cream, and paint a few odd chairs in a slightly paler lime green (4).

Complete the look with colourful zesty accessories and, of course, a few funky cacti in pots.

Desert *rose*

Warm yellows sit easily next to each other, and their warmth makes them perfect for a room that is naturally very cool or doesn't get much natural light. Yellow is a good reflector of sunlight, so it will make a dark room appear lighter and brighter.

A glorious range of yellows to emit light and warmth.

1

2

3

Implement this glowing, golden scheme and bring artificial sunshine into any room.

In a lounge, paint the walls in warm sandstone (1) and carpet in contrasting rich gold ochre (5). Upholster furniture in a stripe fabric of beach yellow (2) and vanilla fudge (3), adding beautiful woven cushions in hues of pale orange (4) and gold ochre.

4

5

When dressing windows, remember to keep curtains bright and light, making sure they don't block out the natural daylight.

Calming *classics*

A thoroughly modern look with a crisp, classic edge.

White – crisp, clean and fresh – is often seen as a clinical colour, but it works particularly well with yellow. This palette really capitalizes on the harmonious relationship of these two hues, creating a scheme that works especially well in a family kitchen.

1

2

3

For a minimal but classic country kitchen, try painting all cupboards and woodwork in pure white (2), and finish with timeless brass handles. Include matching taps in brass also. Use pure white and metallic grey (5) as the colours for a sleek marble worktop.

4

For a sunny backdrop, paint the walls in pale gold (1). The warm tones of this shade will contrast nicely with the cooler tones of the marble.

5

Pick out pieces of ceramic, storage jars and dinnerware in warm clay (3), banana (4) and metallic grey to finish.

Interior *paradise*

Certain colours evoke different feelings or moods. You can instantly create a mood by changing the colour of a room. Where you want to feel relaxed and comfortable stick to a good base of warm neutrals that can be taken as a staple through to other rooms.

The simplest way to update your home is with colour.

When working with a warm yellow neutral such as pale gold (1), use beige tones like natural stone (2) and dark stone (3) to complement it, perhaps as a carpet that runs through from the lounge to the hall, tying the rooms together.

To add depth and a flash of colour pick out prints and woven fabrics in midnight (4) and natural stone, which will look great next to pale gold.

For a contemporary twist to the scheme, include pieces of furniture in herb (5) and shiny chrome to give the relaxed scheme some glamour.

Arabian *nights*

Earthly colours and bold prints for an exotic den.

The colours and trends of the Arabian way of life are the inspiration behind this scheme: bold prints, sumptuous drapery and ambient lighting effects against a beautiful scenic backdrop. For your interior, pull influence from Arabic styling but don't make it look like a stage set.

1

2

3

4

5

A base colour of sand dune (1) allows you to be really creative with colours and patterns. Complement sand dune walls with other earthy neutrals such as natural stone (2) and green clay (3). This unobtrusive backdrop can be accentuated with flashes of strong colour; use gamboge (4) and copper rust (5) in a large striped rug in the centre of the room or as the colours for a block-printed throw or window shade.

Accessorize with candles and lanterns fitting to the theme.

Bedouin *silks*

Staying with the Arabian theme, this scheme takes reference from the nomadic desert tribe of the Bedouin. Evoke the exotic feel of a Bedouin tent with layered throws, woven cloths with metallic threads and bolster cushions strewn across a large dark-wood bed.

Natural silks and velvets for a plush feel to the bedroom.

Like the desert surrounding the tent, paint the walls in sand dune (1), and as a centrepiece find a decadent red mahogany (3) bed.

Scour specialist stores for unusual cushions in purple (4) and deepest peacock (5) embellished with shiny details in metallic pink (2). Use offcuts of velvets and silks to make more cushions and throws.

Choose a woven burlap flooring in sand dune or a shade darker to give a neutral backdrop to the tactile fabrics around the room.

Moving *landscape*

Similarly toned colours for a flawless interior scheme.

Natural light has a dramatic effect on the landscape, from the crisp white light of the morning to the moody softness of dusk. Artificial light has a similar effect, and this must be taken into account when selecting an interior colour scheme.

1

2

3

Colours respond to light, so when choosing a colour paint a small test area first and observe throughout the day and at night; you may find it looks completely different at certain times.

4

Desert cream (1) is a perfect neutral to base the scheme around. Use old white (4) for woodwork and pick a floor covering in desert cream.

5

In a lounge, use combinations of pastel lemon (2), celadon (3) and light teal (5) for upholstery and soft furnishings, and curtain with simple voiles in old white to make the best of the natural light.

Limitless *ground*

The taupe family is extensive, and this scheme takes its colour inspiration from those shades and the natural world around us. Team these natural shades with a range of materials and textures for a stunning, truly decadent bedroom.

Add natural materials to a neutral scheme for timeless elegance.

1

2

3

For a boutique bedroom, paint walls in desert cream (1), and curtain in weighty, full-length drapes in a textured taupe-green (2) fabric.

Choose good-quality cotton bedding in either pure white or a mix of desert cream and sand taupe (3).

4

Furniture should be dark in contrast, either almost black or walnut. Upholster a bedroom stool or statement chair in yellow-cream (4), and place a fabulous moleskin (5) velvet cushion on the seat. Add cushions in the same shade to the bed.

5

Moroccan dreams

Picture mud hut villages nestled in a sun-soaked landscape, clear skies, rolling mountains scattered with delicate flowers and lost worlds dotted with Bedouin tents and colourful textiles. This chapter takes inspiration from the Moroccan way of life and uses a range of earth oranges to harmonize and warm a number of different interior spaces.

Thé à la menthe

This mix of exotic colours would suit a bedroom or lounge.

In Morocco, drinking tea with family and friends is an important ritual. The locals drink incredibly sweet mint tea from beautiful shot-type glasses that are often gilded or coloured—a delicious colour combination that is the inspiration for this scheme.

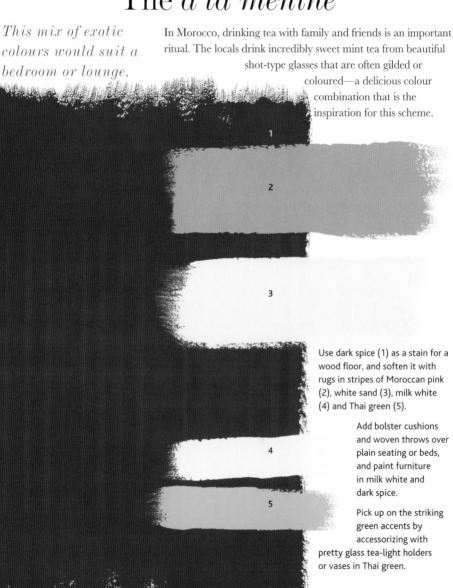

Use dark spice (1) as a stain for a wood floor, and soften it with rugs in stripes of Moroccan pink (2), white sand (3), milk white (4) and Thai green (5).

Add bolster cushions and woven throws over plain seating or beds, and paint furniture in milk white and dark spice.

Pick up on the striking green accents by accessorizing with pretty glass tea-light holders or vases in Thai green.

Ancient *origins*

These orange neutrals are reminiscent of the desert and the subtle colour changes it can produce. An image springs to mind of a Berber village that appears from nowhere through the dunes. Let these colours take you back in time and transport you to an ancient world.

A warm, smart scheme to capture the mystical allure of Morocco.

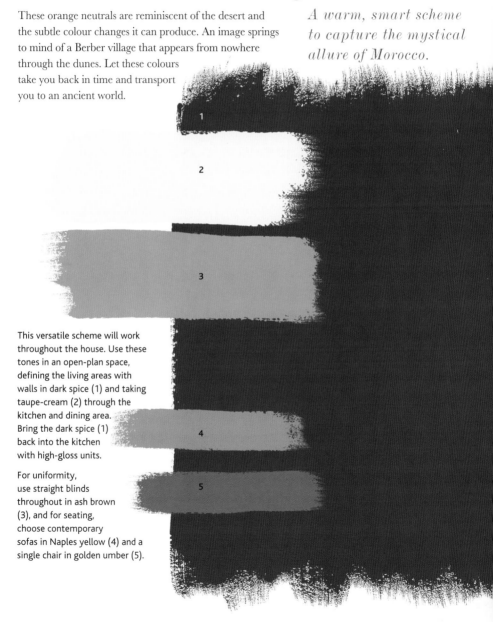

This versatile scheme will work throughout the house. Use these tones in an open-plan space, defining the living areas with walls in dark spice (1) and taking taupe-cream (2) through the kitchen and dining area. Bring the dark spice (1) back into the kitchen with high-gloss units.

For uniformity, use straight blinds throughout in ash brown (3), and for seating, choose contemporary sofas in Naples yellow (4) and a single chair in golden umber (5).

Natural *pigments*

Use these basic tones in a contemplative study or home office.

In the past, pigments were made by grinding minerals and plants, which meant that colours were limited and some very expensive to produce. Today, pigments are made from chemicals, resulting in a kaleidoscope of colours, but this scheme is inspired by the earlier varieties.

Go back to the very roots of colours; use Berber brown (1) and deep amber (3) as a striped or checked carpet, and paint the walls in cinnamon peach (2). Make simple blinds for the windows in Berber brown.

Use mineral (4) for an industrial-style desk, complemented by a steel blue (5) chair.

To finish, frame a range of sepia images in mineral frames and hang in sets on the walls.

Moorish *charm*

The intense decoration and workmanship of existing Moorish architecture is an incredible site to behold. One of the most impressive examples is the Alhambra in Granada, Spain, which hides many surprises in its infinite palaces and palatial gardens and is the inspiration for this colour palette.

The perfect scheme for a retro-styled interior.

1

2

3

The surprise in this scheme is the injection of fiery hot orange (5), which works fabulously as an accent in a retro lounge.

Choose stylish low leather sofas in Berber brown (1), and keep the walls in the background discreet by painting them with ivory (2).

4

Use nude (3) for a carpet, and in the centre of the room, place a huge rug featuring tones of pot pink (4) and hot orange.

5

Finish with a quirky arc lamp with a hot orange shade.

Chasing *gold*

Golden tones add warmth to a dull room or apartment.

Gold has been highly valued since prehistoric times. Associated with wealth, riches, coinage and jewellery, gold readily forms alloys with many other metals, and in a similar way it bonds well with many other hues. Various tones of gold work beautifully well with the browns selected here.

1

2

3

Use peach butter (3) in a carpet that runs through the whole ground floor. Paint all wall space in raw sienna (1).

Pick clean-lined pieces of furniture – retro and new – in mahogany (5), which will look great next to the raw sienna walls and peach butter carpet (3). Upholster a main piece of furniture in yellowed gold (2), use this as your focal point and accessorize with shades of milk chocolate (4).

4

5

For a contemporary twist, add modern prints or mirrors in gold frames.

Earthy *imagination*

Orange is a creative colour that is bursting with energy. Its spectrum is huge, from fiery blood oranges to the deep chestnut browns of the earth. As with many other colours, the appearance of this shade will be influenced by the colours it is grouped with. When placed with calmer neutrals, raw sienna will appear as a rich orange.

Energetic shades to create a flexible and fun environment.

Implement this scheme in a teenager's lounge or children's playroom.

Use raw sienna (1) as your base colour on the walls. Flooring would work in chocolate caramel (3), and woodwork or any permanent details in the lighter calico (2).

For seating use chalk cream (4), and accessorize with Roman clay (5) and raw sienna cushions and beanbags. Similarly, use these shades for bedding and accompanying cushions for a bedroom setting.

House *of green mint*

*Bring the heat
of Morocco into
your bedroom.*

Evoke the feel of a Moroccan villa hidden within the lush foliage
of a hot, arid landscape surrounded by fountains and trickling
water that cool and calm the
senses in the hot desert sun.
This is the perfect paradise
to recreate in a bedroom.

1

2

3

Paint the walls of your bedroom
in spicy amber (1), letting the
warm glow envelop the room.
Add painted furniture in the
contrasting silver-white (2) and
a beautiful silk headboard in
flagstone grey (3).

4

5

Hang flowing lengths
of luxurious spicy amber
and menthe (5) sheers
at the windows and a
deep green leaf (4)
shade inside for practical
privacy.

Crisp, fresh bed linen in silver-
white will make for an inviting
bed, which can be accessorized
with cushions in any one or a
combination of these shades.

Arabic *exoticism*

When echoing a period or a culture in home decoration, take elements of the theme rather than a picture-book copy. Play with scales and contrast to make something ordinary into something unique. For instance, put large floor lamps either side of a bed instead of nightstands and bedside lamps.

Calm neutrals to accentuate spicy Arabian shades.

1

2

3

Use spicy amber (1) as the colour for two large Arabic urns either side of a pinked grey (2) coloured fireplace. Paint the walls in soothing lavender water (3), and cover the floor in natural stone (4).

A spicy warm gold (5) will make a gorgeous sofa tone; keep it low and against the wall like banquette seating, and cover in cushions of various textures that echo all of these selected colours.

4

5

Finally, treat windows by dressing them in curtains or blinds in pinked grey (2).

Foreign *spices*

Bring the flavours of Africa into your kitchen.

When you visit a North African country, the abundance of spices is awe inspiring. The flavours and colours of the cuisine are mouthwatering, and the taste sensation leaves you wanting more. Use this scheme to incorporate these foreign flavours into your home.

1

2

3

Use Moorish orange (1) to clad your kitchen walls in spice. With such a strong colour on the walls it's a good idea to keep the kitchen itself plain, with units in soft butter cream (4). Contrast these light kitchen units with a glorious dark green-brown (3) floor.

4

5

Tagine orange (2) would make a great surprise colour for trendy leather breakfast stools, while calmer pale butternut (5) blinds would punctuate the Moorish orange walls. Include cookware in tagine orange and green-brown tones.

Mysterious *Marrakech*

To instill mystery in a design you need to add elements that people want to know more about or things they don't understand or expect. To do this with an interior, use old pieces of furniture, quirky antique objects and interesting artworks, or even try using old trunks as coffee tables.

Unusual objects and unique furniture for a touch of mystery.

1

2

3

Use Moorish orange (1) as a focal point for a huge abstract painting that almost fills a wall. Paint the walls themselves in duck egg (4) – this will contrast beautifully with the painting.

Find retro black (5) sofas that are sculptural and smart, and for side tables use an old hatbox or perhaps a set of small wooden steps.

4

5

For curtaining and accessories use a combination of rust rose (3) and orange-cream (2) in varying textures and finishes.

Moorish *romance*

A mix of sensual colours and fabrics for the bedroom.

For a seductive, oriental space, step straight out of a Moroccan souk and create a romantic terracotta and sand bedroom or snug. To accentuate the sensual environment, be sure to make the most of a range of plush, sexy fabrics.

1

2

3

As your backdrop, paint walls in sandstorm (1) and combine with billowing voiles in glorious yellow-cream (2).

Use over-the-top exotic decoration with a huge buttoned headboard in luxurious dark taupe (3) silk, with a bed covered in silk cushions in nude (4) and Roman pink (5).

4

5

Hang Moroccan jewelled star lanterns either side of the bed for romantic bedside lights that will project the geometric shapes when turned on.

Mediterranean *colour*

In the arid desert landscape, beautiful Moroccan interiors are filled with explosions of colour. A popular colour is blue, and often a single feature, such as a door or table, is painted in this colour, which resonates in and contrasts with the yellowed oranges and pinks that Morocco is so famous for.

Bold, playful colours perfect for children.

1

2

3

In a playroom, replicate this beautiful sunny Med blue (2) with a painted or high-gloss storage cupboard in which you can throw all the toys and games. Surround the cupboard with a wall painted sandstorm (1).

Add footstools and beanbags in Naples red (3) and Med blue as multifunctional seating. Keep the woodwork and ceilings in off-white (4).

4

5

For a bit of fun and interaction, paint a reachable area of wall space in blackboard (5) paint so the children can draw on the wall.

Sunset *at Essaouira*

A scheme to evoke the warmth of traditional Morocco.

The ancient city of Essaouira, peacefully nestled on the Atlantic coast, is a popular tourist destination in Morocco. The city has many boutique hotels created from Moroccan "riads", traditional dwellings centred around a courtyard and reminiscent of Roman villas.

1

2

3

The rich, warm colours of this scheme take inspiration from these traditional Moroccan communities. In a kitchen with a living or dining area extending to the yard, paint the kitchen area in Sahara sand (1) and the rest of the space in paler grey light (2). Use a natural stone (3) flooring throughout to tie the two spaces together.

4

5

Keep a bare deep brick (5) wall as a feature in a farmhouse-style kitchen, and accessorize with vases and planters in warm pink blush (4) and Sahara sand.

Mosaic *dream*

As a largely practical room, sometimes the bathroom doesn't get as much attention as other rooms in the home. Moroccan bathrooms, however, are both practical and luxurious, using muted sandstones, plaster-wash walls and subdued lighting. Take inspiration from this and treat your bathroom to a Moroccan makeover.

Bring your bathroom to life with bold colours and mosaics.

1

2

3

Arch a pillared opening onto a sunken tub and paint the back wall in the darkest colour, cedar (3). For the face of the arch and the rest of the room, paint a light wash of Sahara sand (1) over white (2). This will ensure the room remains light and airy.

4

For the shower, create a wet-room area with a simple glass screen, then find some beautiful handmade mosaic tiles in violet wash (4) and oxide green (5). Add some glass and antique brass wall lanterns either side of a large mirror edged in the mosaics.

5

Desert *storm*

A combination of exotic desert hues and serene neutrals.

Desert storms can be fierce, violent and noisy, but they are often preceded and succeeded by a period of calm. To create a tranquil, secret escape from the hustle and bustle of everyday life, employ this colour scheme in a living area and hint simply at a few chosen items from Moroccan life.

1

2

3

4

5

Use a pale palette of neutral colours and only the finest natural materials. Fill your lounge with an L-shaped sofa in butternut (1), as large as the room will allow. Paint walls in white sand (3) and carpet in a plush pale taupe (2). Place large floor cushions around and against the sofa in Saharan gold (4) and rust rose (5), and try not to add too much more furniture.

Curtain in butternut raw silk that billows on the floor, and hang on wrought-iron poles. Finish by adding abstract images on large canvases in sandy tones.

Concealed *paradise*

Wander around the mysterious streets of Marrakech and you would never know the beauty that lies beyond the high walls. Walk through an indiscriminate arch and you enter a courtyard garden surrounded by arch-covered walkways leading off to beautiful, palatial rooms.

A royal master suite with a contemporary Moroccan feel.

1

2

3

Paint the room in butternut (1), and add wooden shutters at the windows in chameleon (3).

Upholster the bed and any seating in sandy cream (2) linen or cotton. Cover the bed in orange-cream (4) and gorgeous souk yellow (5) cotton throws, and use the same colours for luxurious silk cushions.

4

5

Complete this contemporary look with dark-wood and rattan furniture and a selection of authentic accessories in orange-cream and chameleon.

Wilderness

Lost in a deep, dark forest, with mile upon mile
of dense woodland and undergrowth—brown is the
colour of the wilderness. Naturally found as the colour
of leather, wood and earth, it is a stable tone that works
in an abundance of situations. It is a practical and
useful colour for the home and sits well with hints of
blue and green, as well as spicier reds and yellows.

Primitive *lines*

Brown is a common tone in contemporary neutral schemes.

Brown is a great, rich staple colour, reminiscent of wood and leather. The colour of the earth and abundant in nature, brown is less harsh than black and works fabulously as the darker component of a modern scheme, bringing warmth to any room.

1

2

3

4

5

The base colour for this palette, exquisitely rich bitter chocolate (1), is incredibly versatile. It works incredibly well with contrasting bright accents for a modern look, or with understated neutrals for timeless elegance.

In an entrance hall, use the bitter chocolate for a few key items of furniture, such as a console table and old leather chair. Paint the walls in light rain (2) to freshen up the space, with army green (3) and taupe (5) curtains or blinds.

Position a pair of lamps or vases in pink clay (4) and taupe to lift the dark furniture.

Scorched *earth*

Browns are warm and earthly, pinks lively and feminine. Pink loves brown and brown loves pink, so mix the natural qualities and earth tones of browns with warm pinks, and combine with luxurious fabrics and textures for a beautiful, romantic bedroom.

Browns and pinks are perfectly balanced in a romantic bedroom.

1

2

3

Base your design around a fabulous wallpaper or fabric in tones of silver-pink and bitter chocolate (1). Paper the bedside wall or hang panels of fabric behind the bed for a more sumptuous feel.

Choose select pieces of furniture in bitter chocolate to set off the pink, and a plain fabric in silver-pink (2) for window blinds.

4

5

Paint the remaining walls in pale, dreamlike cloud (3), and introduce tones of fiery ginger (4) and warm red spice (5) in accessories, such as lamps, ceramics and other textiles.

African *safari*

Layer tones, patterns and natural textures for a modern lounge.

There is a certain theme or style associated with the word "safari": khaki-coloured clothing, pith helmets and animal skin. While this scheme steers clear of animal prints, it does take reference from these colours and the natural tones of the African wilderness.

1

2

3

4

5

A versatile set of colours that can be used in a range of different ways; contrast the lighter colours of white (2) and calico (4) with the harsher brown tones of deep chestnut (1) and barely black (3). Use a single colour, perhaps tarragon (5), as a bold accent to these true neutrals.

Layer the look on a sofa, picking the main upholstery fabric in deep chestnut linen and adding textured cushions in barely black cotton, calico silk, and white felt. Add a simple tarragon throw on the arm.

Animal *tones*

The land of sunlight, wildlife, and scenic grandeur, Africa conjures up powerful images. Imagine the heat, a seemingly endless landscape, a leopard pursuing a wildebeest, or a pack of lions feasting on their catch. Take inspiration from the colours and design of animal skins, but take care not to overdo it.

Use the elements of animal print for a wild design.

1

2

3

Cover one wall, or area of wall, in a textured paper, or paper-backed fabric, that echoes an animal print in rich deep chestnut (1).

Set off this fabulous feature with bright grey (4) contemporary simple furniture. Add a flash of vibrant deep amber (2) in the form of a single large cushion, abstract picture or chair.

4

5

Finish the design with soft fabrics in simple plains or weaves using the subtle tones of peach-orange (3) and maroon (5).

Nature *untouched*

For inspired colour choices, simply look out of the window.

A single leaf in autumn may be all the inspiration you need. Take note of how yellows, browns and greens mingle together in the garden to form a beautiful and perfectly balanced scene, and echo these tones for a sunny open-plan kitchen.

1

2

3

Use tiles in energizing green stone (4), and paint the remaining wall space in gold tint (2). Accentuate the green tones with crisp, fresh striped cotton curtains in olive (5) and gold tint.

4

5

Choose burnt umber (1) as the colour for a chunky kitchen table and kitchen units. This may darken and close the room slightly, but you can lighten and bring sunshine into the room by including worktops and matching chairs in rising sun (3).

To finish, include cookware and bright, pretty dinnerware in any of the accent colours.

Natural *texture*

Dark browns aren't the obvious choice for bathrooms, but bathroom furniture in burnt umber can look sophisticated and sleek against pale neutrals such as almond white and voile. A thoughtfully designed bathroom in these colours will look stunning.

The perfect scheme for a classic, regal bathroom.

1

2

3

Choose a beautiful traditional wood vanity unit in burnt umber (1) with a chunky natural stone top in voile (3). Keep tiles neutral in a similar tone to the voile.

Paint the remaining wall space in almond white (2), and for the window dressing, pick out a striped fabric in apricot cream (5) with a narrow Amazon blue (4) stripe running through it.

4

5

Include an assortment of fluffy towels in almond white and apricot cream, and finish with a woven wicker laundry basket in either almond white or burnt umber.

Deserted *beach*

Take inspiration from a beach walk.

Walking for hours along a deserted beach is an exhilarating experience, allowing you time to contemplate. You can make meaningful keepsakes of a trip to the beach: photograph your children's foot- and handprints in the sand, and hang them up the stairs or in a hallway.

1

2

3

Employ this natural, energizing scheme within your home and capture the invigoration of the great outdoors.

Paint the walls in clay (1) and pick out a feature wall in garden green (4), using this hue as the backdrop to your photo gallery. Frame the images from your beach trip in tones of white clay (2) and dark mud (3) and hang.

4

5

Use khaki brown (5) for flooring that will complement the greens and neutrals. In an entrance hall you may want to include some tall floor vases in white clay.

Earth *water*

The decoration of a home office should be as carefully considered as any other room in the home to ensure it is a pleasant place to work. This scheme centres around bold accents of blue – a colour associated with calm and clear thinking, and thus ideal for a working environment.

Brown tones accented with perky blues to cheer up a workspace.

1

2

3

Starting with a base colour of clay (1) for the walls, choose homely storage such as painted wood furniture in fresh spring water (3) shelved with boxes and files in deeper tones, such as peppermint (2) and bitter chocolate (5). The warm tones of the browns will sit wonderfully well with these cool accents of varying intensities.

4

5

Instead of choosing a conventional desk, find a small table in natural (4) wood and use a comfortable upholstered chair in beautiful, fresh peppermint.

Hermit's *cove*

Sensual, comforting and warming shades evoke relaxation.

At times we all need an escape—a chance to get back to nature and a simpler way of life. Take inspiration from the life of a hermit; implement this warm, cozy group of colours in a snug or quiet corner of your home, and enjoy some relaxing time alone.

1

2

3

4

5

Pick out a wallpaper with a floral design in gorgeous silver birch (1) and wild rose (4) for at least one wall, and paint the remaining walls in silver birch.

Choose a velvety sofa or daybed in neutral taupe (3) cushioned with rich ivory (2) and muted dogwood (5). Layer textures wherever possible; this will further the sumptuous, cozy feel of the room.

Turn off the main lights and use lamps with dogwood shades that diffuse the light.

Wood *love*

One of nature's great fruits, the varying textures and colours of wood mean it has always featured prominently in home decoration. If you love the natural feel and tones of wood use them. Mix antique with new, blond with dark and smooth with rough.

Complementary or contrasting wood tones work well together.

1

2

3

In a dining room, make the focal point a wooden table in teak (5) stain, and dress the centre with wooden vases or accessories in mud (2) tones. Complement this with a dark-wood sideboard.

Upholster chairs in pale olive (3) with mud stained legs. Keep things simple: let the wood do the talking and paint the walls in neutral silver birch (1).

4

5

Add simple accessories, such as a pair of ceramic lamps in white clay (4), which will look great against the wood and silver birch backdrop.

Breaking *ice*

A mix of warm and cool for a masculine bedroom.

The word "ice" is somewhat contradictory in a section that centres around the warm tones of the wilderness, but this scheme is about contrast. Surround khaki with the complementary but cooler tones of lilacs and blues in a luxurious bedroom that is sensual but innately masculine.

1

2

3

Pick out a beautiful, subtle wallpaper, perhaps with metallic hints, in shades of white-lilac (2) and khaki (1). Against this, place rich dark furniture in mud (3), for example, in the form of a stunning contemporary four-poster bed.

4

Hang generous lengths of fabulous flowing silk in regal blue (4) and steel blue (5) at the windows.

5

Upholster a chaise longue in the corner of the room in a silk or velvet khaki fabric, with a beautiful patterned cushion in tones of steel blue and white-lilac.

Snow *crystals*

Browns are wonderful shades for cozy living rooms – they bring warmth into any room – although they can also darken and close a space. Use the contrasting crisp white accents of this palette to balance the scheme and inject a light, fresh feel.

Warm up snowy whites and wintry greys with warm brown tones.

Khaki (1) is a perfectly behaved deep neutral that works well for walls, furniture and upholstery. In a grown-up lounge, use it as a main paint colour with panels of white (3) silk adorning a single wall. This will reflect light and brighten the room.

In front of the white panelling place a warm stone (5) sofa in a vintage leather or suede material.

Accent the room with white furniture and accessories in soft lavender (4) and iced grey (2). Glass tables and lamp bases would also complement nicely.

New *dawn*

Furnishings need not be restricted to interiors.

Opening the curtains to reveal a glorious new dawn is a joy. As sunlight spills into the room, we are drawn to the outside. This beautiful selection of colours invites you to take the beauty of the inside outside. Modern weather-resistant fabrics and furniture allow you to extend your colour palette and design ideas to your yard or balcony.

1

2

3

Choose hard-wearing rattan or wicker furniture in ginger root (1), and soften it up with masses of different cushions, some of them large enough to double as floor cushions and in a vibrant colour such as pink glow (2). Put a pergola in brown stone (5) over the seating area, with a gorgeous canopy in natural light (4).

4

5

Place muted mahogany (3) glass storm lanterns all around, and light with candles when the evenings creep in and the sun disappears.

Hot *sands*

Moving to the warmer orange-based browns and reminiscent of an exotic, hot, arid landscape, this scheme centres around yet more natural, earthly tones. The palette emits warmth, but the boldness of ginger root and nectar could be used in a fun and exciting way to suit a family-friendly living space.

Spice up a neutral base with warm oranges and yellows.

Use ginger root (1) as a practical paint colour, with large sofas in a hard-wearing nectar (5) fabric. Fill the centre of the room with a fun rug in tones of honeysuckle (2), beige (3), nectar and ginger root, and pick chunky tables and sideboards in dark wood (4), with plenty of cupboards and drawers.

Be creative with lighting and hang three large pendants at differing heights in the centre of the room, one in honeysuckle; one in dark wood and the last in nectar, so the space feels designed but also fun and approachable.

White *smoke*

Mix smoky greys and brighter accents for a modern kitchen.

A paler version of khaki, bamboo is another very good neutral that can transcend numerous colour schemes and applications. In this scheme the hue is teamed with a mix of both warm and cool accents for a sleek, contemporary kitchen.

1

2

3

Paint cupboards in ash (2) and try cool silver-green (3) as a tile colour. These colours will look fantastic against bamboo (1) coloured walls.

Moving into the dining area of the kitchen, deepen the wall colour to dark stone (4). This will intensify the space in a gentle way.

4

5

Choose ash blinds for the windows with a shot of silver-green, and add ember (5) accessories sparingly.

Quiet *noise*

Neutral tones are easy to live with and can evolve into different schemes or styles easily, so it is possible to have a base neutral that runs throughout the house. By simply changing accent colours it's possible to change the whole feel of a room.

Make an impact without being garish.

1

2

3

In an open-plan space, keep the basic upholstery in bamboo (1) and furniture in warm black (5).

Make simple Roman blinds for the windows in natural (2) fabric, and add a honey (3) and warm black rug to centralize the seating space and make it a real feature of the room.

4

Add a large floor vase in kidney bean (4), and on the other side of the room, place a smaller kidney bean lamp on a table to mirror the larger one.

5

Handmade *fabric*

Neutrals and natural materials walk hand in hand.

Natural materials are not perfect and will invariably have flaws and imperfections. But if you love their true textures and how they look and behave, then use them in your interiors regardless, as these imperfections can add to their charm and will lead to a unique finished look.

1

2

3

In a lounge or living area, use hemp (1) as the base for your wall colour, and hang simple true calico (2) curtains from beautiful wooden poles in grey-green (5) at the window.

4

Pick out a natural seagrass or wood floor in a hemp shade, and use moody eggplant (4) as a natural dyed fabric for sofas and seating.

5

For added texture and a touch of luxury in the scheme, add cushions in silk (3) and grey-green velvet.

Frayed *edge*

When designing a room you may feel the need to be symmetrical, neat and ordered. Employing a scheme will no doubt have you striving for perfection, but just remember that not everything has to be perfect. Distressed finishes can look smart and work well in a bedroom or lounge.

Discard perfection for a unique, lived-in look.

1

2

3

Use hemp (1) as a wall colour, providing a neutral base for distressed furniture. Paint the furniture in warm stone (2) and give it a distressed finish. Use another neutral, dark stone (3) as a floor covering, whether carpet, wood or seagrass.

4

Nudging toward pink, cover an old chair in a distressed dusky pink (4) fabric, and hang curtains in brown-pink (5) on distressed warm stone curtain poles.

5

Keep lighting low and diffused with floor and table lamps, rather than a main central fitting.

Starry *night*

Incorporate elements of the night sky in a contemporary kitchen.

When the clouds clear, the midnight blue sky is a natural wonder that twinkles with bright metallic stars. Perhaps it's the unknown that makes it so magical and alluring. Take inspiration from the night sky with this thoroughly modern kitchen.

1

2

3

Choose ecru (1) as a base colour for kitchen units, and use night sky (4) as a contrasting tone for all worktops. Paint walls in a mix of soft bark (2) and white (3), pinpointing where you want your eye to be led with the soft bark.

4

Keep flooring natural in lighter shades of either ecru or soft bark.

5

To complete the scheme, accessorize with light fixtures, handles and other finishing touches in burnished nickel (5) for a sleek, modern feel.

Breaking *daylight*

Hazy tones are what make neutrals work, crossing the line from a true colour into an ambiguous description. Is it grey, green or beige? Ecru is a deliciously soft and amiable neutral, edging toward brown with a hint of pink, making it a versatile shade. Team with light accents to recreate the feel of the morning haze.

A fresh, sunny look for a modern lounge.

1

2

3

In a lounge, carpet the floor in ecru (1) with flecks of olive (4), and paint or paper the walls in ecru also.

Choose olive for main pieces of upholstered furniture and accent them with highlights of yellow sand (5) and green haze (3).

4

Hang a large central pendant with an olive shade in the centre of the room, and mix painted furniture in buff (2) with wooden pieces in oak.

5

Any of these accent shades will be perfect for soft furnishings and accessories, so experiment.

Ice cream

The prettiest of all tones, pink is typically used in
feminine interior spaces. To avoid getting too sickly
sweet, mix these shades with moody greys and stony
neutrals. Soft, warm and comforting, the gentle, relaxed
tones of these milky ice-cream colours are perfect for
living spaces and for promoting sweet dreams.

Black *cherry*

Rich cherry accented with cool shades for an elegant bedroom.

Inspired by the deep colour of a bulging bunch of black cherries, this scheme combines a real mix of hues. The cool tones of pink-grey perfectly complement indulgent, intense black cherry, and make for a flawless scheme .

For an expressive black cherry (1) bedroom let slinky silk and vibrant velvets collide, while keeping the walls and flooring neutral in stone white (4).

Make a huge oversized buttoned headboard in black cherry velvet, and layer the bed with sumptuous silks and satins in varying tones of pink-grey (2, 3).

Hang lengths of black cherry silk at the windows, and keep furniture to a minimum in expensive-looking dark oak (5).

Blackcurrant *sorbet*

Choosing to be adventurous with colour in a kitchen can really pay off. The kitchen is the room that families probably spend the most time in, and it is increasingly becoming the main living area. Employing these colours in a carefully designed scheme will give you a kitchen to be proud of.

Strong colours in a spacious kitchen make a real statement.

For a real difference, use black cherry (1) for bold kitchen units with a contrasting bespoke toughened-glass worktop and backsplash in orchid (2).

Keep the walls neutral with a warming shade of light stone (3). A floor covering in this same shade, or one with a similar intensity, will prevent the room from becoming too dark or closed in. Accent with hints of deep blackcurrant (4) and green stone (5) in any soft furnishings and accessories.

Summer *berries*

Berry-inspired colours to inject warmth into a room.

The components of this palette are bold, bright and daring. There is no doubt that they will warm a cold or large room, but play with balance when using shades that are all quite robust, making sure you don't use the colours in equal measure, otherwise the effect could feel heavy and over the top.

1

2

3

In a chilly lounge or drawing room, paper or paint the walls in mulberry (1) and the woodwork in soothing vanilla cream (2).

Use gorgeous vanilla bean (3) as a floor covering; in a cold room, a soft carpet would be best.

4

5

For main sofas or seating use khaki green (4), and for the odd occasional chair pick a different fabric in bramble fruits (5).

Accessorize with any of the accent shades, and add plenty of mirrors to maximize on light.

Turkish *delight*

Think of the powdery pink icing and fragrant, transparent rose of Turkish delight. To conjure up a concoction of these delicious flavours at home, surround mulberry with subtle pinks in a hallway and create an inviting entrance.

Immerse yourself in the delicate flavours of rose and the mystery of Turkey.

Paint panelling in milky coffee (4) with deep mulberry (1) walls above. Carpet in luxurious, rich cocoa (5) flecked with hints of mulberry; chocolates always work well with pinks.

Add painted furniture in sugar ice (3) and large pendant lampshades in cocoa (5).

To complete the scheme, accessorize with pretty floral prints in sugar ice or milky coffee frames and real flowers in rose water (2) vases.

Fruits *of the forest*

A scheme to unite a conservatory with the rest of the house.

Conservatories are often overlooked as a room in the home because people only use them in the summer months, while the rest of the year they remain shut off from the main house. But a little extra love and decorative consideration will make a conservatory more appealing, so you'll want to use it all year round.

1

2

3

Simple tricks to make a conservatory feel like a part of the house include running the same flooring through from the connecting room or hallway, so it appears as an extension rather than a separate room, and plastering the interior rather than leaving it as brick.

4

5

Paint the plastered walls in warm stone (3) and put down a wooden floor in rich pip (4).

Use lychee (1) as the main colour focus of the room in upholstery, and accent this with chiffon (2) and cherry (5).

Exotic *flavours*

This range of gorgeous, rich tones is offset by the calm, delicate accents of the scheme. To infuse the bedroom with elements of the exotic, paint or paper the walls in lychee and hang oriental prints and fabrics in contemporary box frames painted in pistachio.

Stylized florals and dark lacquer furniture for a lavish look.

For furniture, choose bitter chocolate (3) in a lacquered-wood finish with self-coloured or pistachio (5) handles to further the opulent look.

Choose bedding in rich vanilla bean (2), and find a jade tone such as green marl (4) to mix with lychee (1) for a floral throw and silk cushions. Layering textures and colours will add to the plush feel.

Finish with a bitter chocolate floor vase filled with branches of pussy willow.

Delicate *balance*

A thoughtful mix of pinks for a tasteful kitchen

It is unusual for people to use pinks in an environment such as a kitchen or dining room for fear that it will look too childish or girly. However, when used with restraint, pinks can be very elegant and really enhance a space.

1

2

3

In a kitchen-dining room, keep a theme running from kitchen to dining space by using coffee cream (3) for a wood worktop and wood dining table. Paint a grey-rose (1) wall in the kitchen area and mirror this in the dining space with grey-rose blinds or curtains at the windows. Paint the rest of the wall space in ash (5) to keep it light and fresh.

4

5

Add coffee cream shelves in the kitchen area with pretty lilac-white (4) and plaster pink (2) ceramics displayed or stacked there, as a practical but attractive storage solution.

Elderflower *and rose*

In folklore, the elderflower was supposed to ward off evil influence. Today it is most commonly used in herbal teas or soft drinks. This scheme takes reference from its delicate flavour, combining it with rose for a refreshing, fragrant infusion of colours, perfect for a lounge.

Treat a tired lounge with a mix of pinks and citrus.

1

2

3

Paint walls in grey-rose (1) and for a contemporary feel, use grey-rose with bright, refreshing chartreuse (5) as a striped fabric for a sofa. Carpet the area in dark stone (2) with an elderflower (3) tufted wool rug in front of the seating.

4

Cover a large footstool in zingy lemon cream (4) and use in place of a coffee table. Add curved glass side tables at either end of the sofa, and let a large abstract painting bring all the colours together on the wall.

5

Noisette *twist*

A peachy neutral looks great next to a mix of browns.

The warm tones of brown look fantastic with both oranges and pinks. Butternut pink, is a delightful combination of both colours and will work wonderfully when mixed with a range of brown tones.

1

2

3

To create a contemporary twist in a traditional bathroom, paint the outside of a fabulous roll-top bath in butternut pink (1) and finish with greyed ivory (2) feet.

Set the bath off against a distressed wood floor in brown olive (5), and paint walls in greyed ivory. If you need to tile a shower area or backsplash, choose a glazed pale walnut–colored (4) tile.

4

5

Mix accessories and towels in tones of butternut pink, chestnut (3) and pale walnut, and mount a traditional framed gilt mirror on the wall to reflect light and add a touch of class.

Old *creamery*

Butternut pink is a welcoming and interesting colour choice for a dining room, and, mixed with neutrals such as greyed ivory and light stone, it can create an elegant but relaxed space. Keep decoration simple, with the main focus on the dining table.

In a classic dining room, keep the setting simple.

1

2

3

Paint the walls of the room butternut pink (1) for an inviting backdrop. Choose feature lighting to highlight the warmth of butternut pink; clotted cream (4) wall lights with dark morello (5) silk shades will work fantastically well. Include a matching morello pendant shade for over a wooden morello dining table.

4

5

Accentuate the wall colour further by installing a light stone (3) fireplace mantel with greyed ivory (2) candelabras on each corner. Keep floor covering light, in either greyed ivory or light stone.

English *toffee*

Colours to give an open-plan apartment a homely atmosphere.

In today's modern world, a large part of interior design centres around contemporary style: sleek, sophisticated decor and open-plan spaces. While modern and stylish, it can sometimes be difficult to make large open-plan apartments feel homely. Let this scheme show you how.

Candy (1) is a light-reflecting colour that will give a warm glow to any space. Mix candy on the walls, and include furniture and seating in flat grey (3) and pebbled cream (4).

Carpet or cover the floor in a practical material and colour such as flat cocoa (5), because in an open-plan space it will need to put up with a high level of traffic.

To finish, add a bright injection of colour with flashes of deep pink (2), for example, in the form of a modern lamp in the corner of the lounge.

Crème *caramel*

Sometimes rooms have to be adaptable for multiple uses.
For example, an office cum guest bedroom needs to be efficient
and practical but welcoming and attractive at the same time.
Using neutrals with warm tones and delicate pinks will help
to take the focus away from
working environments.

*A clever scheme to
combine both work
and rest.*

1

2

3

Carpet the room in candy (1) and
paint the walls in clotted cream
(5). Pick a compact sofa bed in
neutral caramel (4) and dress with
mauve grey (2) and beautiful
butternut pink (3) cushions.

Be clever with furniture
and choose a pretty
table rather than a
conventional desk
and a cupboard that can
double as a wardrobe.

4

5

Add shelves painted
in candy, and use rattan
storage boxes to hide stationery
and other work accoutrements.

Strawberry *mousse*

Strawberry cream will gel with most schemes and won't tire or date.

People frequently decorate rooms to update a look. A scheme or look at the height of fashion won't remain there forever. Selecting a scheme that won't date is a challenge, but using a neutral base is normally a good start.

1

2

3

Moving more into browny pinks, strawberry cream (1) is a great base neutral for just about any interior space.

In a lounge, paint walls in strawberry cream, and keep it fresh and light with natural grey (2) floors and linen (3) blinds or shutters at the windows.

4

5

Edge a strawberry cream linen chair with a hazlenut (4) trim for upholstery that's contemporary and fresh. Choose a low-level modern sofa in light teal (5), and add large strawberry cream linen square cushions and smaller hazlenut velvet bolster cushions.

Coffee *bean*

Imagine the delicious aroma of roasted coffee beans. This scheme takes inspiration from the deep, rich brown colour of the beans themselves and the harmonious colour of the red coffee cherries from which they derive. Employ these colours in a family living area.

Use these dark accent shades in a family lounge or children's playroom.

1

2

3

Paint the walls of your chosen room in strawberry cream (1).

For furniture, pick chunky leather sofas in coffee bean (3) to sit on a funky blood orange (5) carpet. Adorn with scatter cushions in shades of cappuccino (2) and pot pink (4). Use these accent shades in a large geometric pattern for blinds or curtains also.

4

5

Add fun beanbags in cappuccino for the children to lounge on and as a practical solution for unexpected visitors.

Thai *magic*

Subtle pink tones punctuated by exotic, vibrant accents.

For a grown-up but decadently girly bedroom for a teenager, use these understated pinks with dark wood furniture. The voluptuousness of pink works perfectly with the richness of the browns, creating an incredibly warming and welcoming room.

1

2

3

Paint the walls of the room in delicate orchid (1), with a feature wall of paper in beautiful opal (2) and cotton candy (5).

Choose a grown-up warm brown (3) bed frame and simple wood furniture in the same finish. Use opal for bed linen and any of the accent colors for cushions.

4

5

Break up the pink by hanging a show-stoppingly large Thai green (4) shade in the centre of the room, and accessorize with strings of lights, Buddha statues and potted orchids.

Eastern *rose*

In this unusual group of colours, the gentle pink tinge of delicate orchid is played down by the use of browny neutrals and blue-toned flint, in a contemporary scheme that would suit an open-plan kitchen area.

A modern scheme that you may not naturally put together.

1

2

3

Paint the walls in delicate orchid (1) and use vanilla (4) and warm cream (3) for kitchen cabinets.

Choose dark stone (5) as a tile or wood tone for flooring to contrast nicely against the light kitchen units. Dark stone would also work as a colour for worktops.

4

Pick out warm cream for simple blinds with dark stone wooden pulls on the bottom, and accessorize with flint (2) ceramics and cookware for a subtle hint of grey-blue.

5

Pink *pistachio*

Soft, creamy tones to promote relaxation.

Emulate the smooth, velvety touch of a petal with pretty pinks and creamy pistachios. This gentle combination will work well in relaxed lounges, but it's also a winner in the bedroom.

1

2

3

Try the combination of peach tint (1) walls and pale pistachio (2) underfoot; the strength of colour is especially similar in these shades, so they will look seamlessly beautiful together.

4

To dress windows, add some rich asparagus (3) and plaster (4) curtains or blinds in a delicate floral or stripe.

5

Mirror the pale pistachio in painted furniture, and add hints of pastel orange (5) and plaster in ceramic vases and accessories.

Flower *water*

Pink is a combination of red and white, but there are so many variants. Pinks can be tinged brown, orange, yellow and grey. Peach tint has a grey edge to it, which makes it a refined and sophisticated pink tone.

Neutrals and hints of pink, perfect for a study or small lounge.

1

2

3

Play it safe and choose natural stone (2) for flooring and paint the walls in peach tint (1). This will keep the room light and airy.

With the walls and floors in these creamy shades, use the bold but elegant tone of mulberry (4) for upholstery with warm cream (3) and pink (5) polka dot cushions.

4

5

Pick out the tone of natural stone as a background colour for a shade with a beautiful, fun pinky pattern.

Vanilla *story*

A pale scheme that will need loving attention to keep it pure.

Vanilla is smooth, tasty and rich. Derived from the orchid, vanilla is also a pungent scent that has been used for centuries in perfumes. It mixes well with most colours and is therefore a highly adaptable hue for decor.

1

2

3

Accentuate the orangey undertones of white-peach (1) with vanilla (4) and white lemon (2) striped cotton sofas.

At the windows hang long drapes that pool on the floor in vanilla silk.

4

Cover the centre of the room with a luscious brown velvet (5) shaggy rug that should feel fabulous under bare feet. Cushion the sofas in mauve hint (3) and white-peach for an understated nod to colour.

5

Peach *melba*

Picture a juicy peach half surrounded in vanilla ice cream and sprinkled with hazelnut shavings. This palette is almost as soft as the last, and so good you can almost taste it. Use this scrumptious peach and pinky scheme as inspiration for a little girl's bedroom.

A delicious set of colours inspired by the classic dessert.

1

2

3

Start with a pretty wallpaper in white-peach (1) and strawberry milk (5). Above a painted orchid (3) daybed drape a cream of peach (2) voile canopy edged with pink beads, stones and crystals.

Add a collection of polka dot, floral and striped pastel cushions in mauve dust (4), strawberry milk, cream of peach and orchid (3).

4

5

To finish, adorn walls with painted hearts, beaded curtains and strings of lights.

Northern lights

The matriarch of all the neutrals, cream works on so many levels. It is light, bright and clean while remaining warm and welcoming. Most Scandinavian interiors are simple and delicate with their colour balance but are still inviting spaces. Use this chapter to take inspiration from Scandinavian design and landscape.

Swedish *modern*

This look works particularly well in an open-plan space.

Infamous for Modernist furniture crafted from natural materials, chiefly wood, Swedish design is beautiful, organic and highly functional. Take inspiration from this style and combine with a fairly simple colour palette for a stunning overall effect.

1

2

3

Paint the walls in blond wood (1) and make simple blinds or curtains in white (2) and country white (3) striped cotton. Pick plain modern sofas in black (5) leather.

4

5

Set off this basic colour palette with some beautiful Swedish modernist antiques in teak (4), or find good contemporary interpretations.

Take care not to over-accessorize. Stick to a set of lamps and a beautifully designed glass or ceramic item.

Atmospheric *light*

The Scandinavian style features bleached woods, whitewashed furniture and gingham and floral textiles with a homemade feel. It can look a little twee if overdone, but if used thoughtfully with these selected colours they will work fantastically well in a dining room.

Take elements of rustic, homely Scandinavian design into your home.

1

2

3

Paint the walls in blond wood (1) and pick out a delicate fabric for window dressings in gorgeous Nordic cream (4).

Paint wooden chairs and a table in a wash of magnolia (5), and add tied-on seat pads in white-grey (2).

4

If you are blessed with an open fireplace, keep the mantel simple and painted magnolia with logs stacked neatly by the side.

5

Decorate the room with ceramics in deep sky (3) and white-gray, and lots of tall church candles.

Beachy *point*

Scandinavian colours are perfect for a beach house or country cottage.

The Scandinavian love of bleached woods and all things natural transcends beautifully to a seaside retreat.

Since most beach houses operate an open-plan living space, in the main sitting room paint the walls in sand (1) and elsewhere in Swedish linen (2) to make the space cozy and relaxing.

1

2

3

Choose reclaimed and Swedish or shaker furniture in wood (4) or painted in white clay (5).

To soften a wood floor, throw down plenty of rugs in various textures and tones of neutrals with hints of a colour such as lilac-white (3). These should look great and feel fabulous under bare feet.

4

5

To complete the look add candles in storm lanterns with sand in the bottom and plenty of soft cashmere throws to keep guests warm once the sun goes down.

Gustavian *styling*

Swedish Gustavian furniture is elegant yet simple. Its look is classic and can transcend both traditional and modern interiors. This group of colours attempts to do the same. Create a dreamy bedroom with an elegant Gustavian chaise longue painted and upholstered in Swedish linen.

A scheme of simple colours and design for a bedroom.

1

2

3

Take sand (1) as a natural colour for a beautiful polished wood or parquet floor that will be the real star next to these muted colors.

Add a hint of glamour with an antique-looking crystal green (5) chandelier hung in the centre of the room.

4

For textiles, mix checks, stripes and plain natural linens and cottons in beige (3), gingham green (4) and Swedish linen (2). Layering fabrics and textures will make the room feel comfy and cozy.

5

Textural *shades*

A scheme that allows you to make the most out of textures.

When working with a basic colour palette or neutrals, introducing texture will ensure the scheme does not become bland or boring. Work with a variety of finishes and materials, such as metals, woods, cottons, linens and natural stones, and experiment to your heart's content.

1

2

3

In a lounge, paint walls in suede (1) and furniture in white (3) with dull steel grey (4) handles.

For sofas, choose a textured woven Nordic cream (2) fabric and place a huge Nordic blue (5) rug in the centre of the room.

4

5

Pick out key items, such as an odd vase or lampshade, in Nordic blue. Add different coloured wooden frames, an upholstered footstool in steel grey suede and some crystal candlesticks for a sleek, sophisticated feel.

Nordic *charm*

Though Scandinavian interiors are generally light and based around white or neutrals, they always manage to look warm and inviting. Conjure up the image of a large open fire; imagine the crackling flames, the warmth that emanates and the cozy feeling this scene creates.

Evoke the relaxing feel of an open fire and the soft light it creates.

1

2

3

To create the same feel, use warm yellowed neutrals in a family room focused around suede (1) coloured walls.

Warm beige (2) makes a practical base colour for upholstery, which can be teamed with cushions in cheery lamplight (3) and muted lemon (4).

4

For a lived-in look, choose storage cupboards and side tables in antique oak (5), and accessorize with interesting but educational items, such as a huge bookcase, prints of old maps or an old globe on a stand.

5

Crystal *light*

*A cool selection
of colours to
maximize light.*

A rainbow of beautiful colours appear when light and crystal react. Take inspiration from this image and brighten up a bathroom with these light-reflecting colours and an over-the-top use of mirrors.

1

2

3

Pick a beautiful natural stone in pinky buff (1) for both floor and wall tiles. Paint any remaining wall space in neutral voile (3). This should keep the room light, airy and fresh.

4

Choose pure, clean white (2) for furniture and sanitary ware.

5

To increase the room's light, source a collection of both new and antique mirrors in varying framed finishes painted silver-grey (4). Use ice blue (5) and silver-grey as the colours for towels and accessories.

Warm *glow*

A traditional Scandinavian folk scheme in a girl's bedroom will make it warm, welcoming and homely. Go back in time with fleece throws, wooden animals, knitted teddy bears and old-fashioned peg boards.

A fun folk scheme to excite any child.

Start by painting the walls of the room in pinky buff (1) and furniture in a white (4) wash.

Choose a wrought-iron black (5) bed and pile it high with cushions in pinky buff and red wash (2) gingham and pale blue (3) and white stripes. With "busy" cushions keep bed linen plain and simple, perhaps in pale blue.

Pick a pretty floral in muted pastels for a seat pad on a small wooden chair in the corner, and use the same fabric for the window dressing.

Milk *and honey*

*Try a lighter,
brighter approach
to the dining room.*

Honey is a fabulous warm neutral; its yellow undertones make it very adaptable and stop it from looking cold. Although a favourite for kitchen schemes and perhaps not the normal choice for a dining room, honey looks great with woods and whitewashed furniture.

1

2

3

Position a large trestle-style white (2) washed and distressed dining table on bleached wood (3) floorboards. This will look great against honey (1) walls.

Use pale iris white (4) to paint wooden chairs in varying shapes and sizes, and place a pair of decorative crystal candlesticks on the dining table.

4

5

For curtains, pick a light cotton voile in iris white and simple wrought-iron poles. For a flash of colour, upholster the seat pads in red wash (5) cotton.

Sweet *surprise*

Picture a jar of sweet and viscous golden honey and you'll see the inspiration behind this scheme. The warm golden yellow is soothing and tranquil and will work in any number of settings but is perfect for a child's nursery because the colour can easily be adapted as the child grows.

Use wholesome honey as a rich, warm base colour.

1

2

3

4

5

Paint the walls in wholesome honey (1), and, in traditional Scandinavian style, keep the furniture painted pure white (5).

Use faded orange (2) to make a loose cover for a small comfortable armchair in the corner of the room, and add a grey-taupe (4) cotton cushion for extra comfort.

Hang a fabric shade for the central light in pale mauve (3), which will diffuse the light to a lovely warm glow. Find simple animal prints and hang on the walls in pure white frames to finish.

Distressed *edge*

*Rough edges and
natural colours
for a rustic look.*

When you choose natural stone for a bathroom or hallway, there are many finishes available. If you want to go streamlined and flush pick a filled and straight-edge tile, but if you want a rustic feel choose a chipped-edge product.

1

2

3

In a large hallway, choose a large tile in heritage cream (1) for the whole length of the hall.

Up the stairs, run a carpet runner in mushroom (5) and ash (2) stripes. Paint the walls in muted birch (3) and curtain simply with gorgeous billowing, floor-length curtains in Nordic cream (4).

4

5

In a bathroom, Nordic cream units will work wonderfully against muted birch tiled or painted walls and a mushroom coloured floor.

Evening *warmth*

If you enjoy a touch of shabby chic, try picking out a pretty floral in neutral colours and combining it with an old leather armchair, fluffy rugs and hand-knitted cushions. These colours combined with a variety of textures will result in a room centred around comfort.

Sometimes a room looks better if it's a little lived in.

1

2

3

Paint the main walls in heritage cream (1) and re-cover an old armchair or sofa in a distressed, hot chocolate (4) leather.

Pick a floral fabric in tinted cream (2) and bleached sun (5) natural linen, and use this to cover cushions.

4

Paint the woodwork and fire surround in natural linen (3), and place picture frames and plants around the room. Use a variety of shapes, sizes and finishes for the accessories, so that they look like they've been collected over time.

5

Looking *for light*

Ideas and colours to make a basement feel more spacious.

If you need to brighten up a basement lounge or workroom, use mirrors to capture and throw light around. Not only do they reflect light, but they also increase the feeling of space. If ceiling height is an issue, which is often the case in basements, use pot lights or wall lights.

1

2

3

Paint all the walls in ivory (1) and follow similarly with white (2) for all the woodwork. At the windows choose uniform blinds or shutters in muslin (4).

For the main upholstery play between ice (3) and ash (5), keeping scale in mind so as not to overpower the space.

4

5

Finally, hang mirrors where they reflect interesting vistas and can bounce around the light from the windows, and bring some low-maintenance plants inside – they'll make the space seem more organic and lived in.

Peaceful *dusk*

To enjoy the view as the last light of day streams through the window, make a quiet spot you can relax in. Position a wrought-iron (4) daybed filled with cushions of all shapes and sizes in the place where you have the best view – perhaps this is a landing or an area in a bedroom.

A range of soft, subtle tints for a restful space.

1

2

3

To ensure the daybed is the focus of the space, keep the surrounding walls neutral in ivory (1), and use dark stone (3) as the colour for floor covering.

Make cushions from soft pink (5) woven linen with mother-of-pearl buttons, dark stone (3) suede, with spots in lilac moon (2), and ivory (1) silk with crystal studs. Use these to add texture to the daybed.

4

5

Position a bookshelf or magazine rack nearby so the area feels like it has a purpose.

Scandinavian *style*

A subtle, Nordic colour palette, perfect for a formal lounge.

Nordic colours are gentle and inoffensive, so they make a great basis for a traditional setting with period detailing, such as a grand marble fireplace and elegant cornice. A muted palette such as this is extremely versatile and will enable you to inject your own styling.

1

2

3

Paint the walls in warm, glorious Nordic cream (1), before washing a wood floor in white (5).

Furnish the room with stonewash (2) upholstery and antique furniture in dark oak (4). Include a range of found objects, such as wooden statues, vases and masks.

4

5

Accessorize and add texture to the scheme with soft furnishings in Nordic cream and lime white (3) cottons and silks.

Natural *lines*

This simple yet serious scheme would work especially well in a modern renovation or open-plan apartment. Use the softness of Nordic cream and the weightier accents of this palette and take the austere modernist style into a contemporary kitchen.

Serious, sophisticated colour choices for a modern kitchen.

Use Nordic cream (1) as your base colour and pick out shiny chrome (4) appliances and hardware.

Choose chrome-legged stools or chairs with black (2) leather seats and contrast light ivory (3) kitchen units with black granite for the worktops.

For a sleek injection of colour choose olive (5) for neat roller or Roman blinds and as a base colour for abstract artworks on the walls.

White heat

Imagine snowflakes falling through the last light of
the day, colours changing through pale yellow and
barely-there pinks and warming the freezing air.
White is sexy yet clean and virginal. Drawing on
all of the colour sections, pick out the lightest
"white" shades in each palette and contrast and
complement the purest of all the neutrals. It is
amazing how the tiniest hint of colour can change
and impact the ambience of a space.

Gentle *whites*

For a calming and personable interior choose fresh neutrals.

Fresh, light and crisp neutrals create a summery scheme that works well all year round. Grey ice is a thoroughly modern shade and makes a great base for these citrus tints of lemon and lime. This pale, contemporary palette choice will help you create an airy, spacious feel in any room.

1

2

3

Introduce the scheme into an open-plan kitchen-dining room, with grey ice (1) walls and lime white (2) painted kitchen units.

Simple, clean grey-white (3) worktops in a natural marble will work well with this scheme, and you can bring focus to the dining or sitting area area by painting a wall in pale lemon (4).

4

5

For non-painted furniture, choose a natural oak (5) finish and a simple shaker style to ensure the scheme stays light and bright.

Masculine *detail*

A plain backdrop will increase the feeling of space within a small property. When space is important you have to be careful with furniture, so be practical and don't try to squeeze in too many pieces or items that are too big. Ideal for a studio apartment or an inner-city crash pad, introducing navy gives a masculine edge to this palette.

Combine neutrals with dark accents for an ultra-sleek scheme.

1

2

3

4

5

Paint the walls in grey ice (1) and carpet throughout in warm, neutral biscuit (3).

For a touch of sleek sophistication choose navy (2) for sofa upholstery and scatter some simple cotton cushions in biscuit and pure white (4).

Finish with black and white prints in large charcoal (5) frames for sharp and stylish yet uncomplicated decoration.

Tonal *change*

A perfect partnership of pinks and greys.

Pinks are warm and inviting, but toned in this way and teamed with greys they can also look modern and chic. To give a contemporary twist to the traditional "girly pink" bedroom, choose a harmonious combination of warm grey-whites and dusky pinks.

1

2

3

Paint the bedhead wall in dark blush (5) and the remaining walls in winter white (1). Paint wooden floorboards in either winter white or light blush (3).

Upholster the headboard in light blush silk and use the same fabric to make dress cushions.

4

Choose good-quality cotton bed linen in orchid white (2) and add texture and a touch of luxury with a sateen bed throw in medium blush (4). Accessorize with glass perfume bottles and silver candlesticks.

5

Natural *stone*

A bathroom should appear clean, fresh and light. If the room is not blessed with a flood of natural sunlight, then you need to implement a scheme that capitalizes on that which is available. Natural stone and neutral whites are simple but effective when creating a light and airy contemporary bathroom.

Keep colours and materials basic for a sophisticated bathroom.

1

2

3

Use winter white (1) marble wall tiles and paint any remaining wall space in pure white (2).

To bring warmth to the room, lay a wood floor in oak (4) and choose free-standing sink units, also in oak.

Make the most of the bright white space by placing a large mirror framed in oak on the largest wall. Mirrors are a great way to maximize a room's light source.

4

5

Accessorize with a range of towels in peached ivory (3), pure white and pale sage (5).

Bright *splash*

Jazz up a neutral kitchen with flashes of vibrant colour.

A great way to make a neutral scheme fun and family-friendly is to add bright, bold injections of colour. If you like to change the feel of a space through the seasons this is an ideal scheme for you, because cushions and accessories can be mixed and matched accordingly.

1

2

3

In a family kitchen or dining area paint the walls in a hard-wearing blush (1) and choose kitchen units in pure white (2), which look particularly great in a high-gloss finish. For flooring opt for hard-wearing seagrass or natural stone (3) tiles.

4

5

Now for the fun part. Cushion alternate chairs in fuchsia (4) and pea green (5), and add brightly coloured ceramic vases and dishes in the same bright shades. Finally, frame your favourite children's pictures in an informal gallery on the gorgeous blush walls.

Calm *neutrals*

Choose natural fabrics such as wool, cotton, linen and silk for an array of furniture and soft furnishings. If you have a fireplace, make it the focal point of the room by positioning seating around the hearth, making it inviting and comfortable.

For a warm and cozy neutral lounge add texture and interest.

1

2

3

Pick a white butter (2) finish for the fireplace, either painted or stone, and paint or paper the walls in blush (1).

Carpet the room in a textured light taupe (3), something that looks and feels great, and use mouse (4) and grey clay (5) as shades for sofas and chairs.

4

5

Dress windows in billowing curtains in either white butter or mouse, and find beautiful mohair throws in blush to rest on the arms of sofas for chilly winter evenings.

Cluster *of pink*

A scheme centred around contrast.

This palette is based around the juxtaposition of light and dark, combining delicate accent tones with startling darks. Mixing extreme tones in this way has dramatic effects – perfect for a striking and contemporary living room.

1

2

3

For a pretty Japanese cherry-blossom-inspired room, make the star a pair of buttermilk (3) sofas. Choose velvet or silk for a glamorous edge, or stick to woven cotton for a "daytime" look.

As a neutralized platform for the creamy furniture, choose a warm grey (4) carpet and colour walls in subtle rose-white (1).

4

5

Complete the look with Oriental-style dark wood or lacquered furniture in barely black (5) and accessories in white (2) and barely black.

Modernity *personified*

As the resurgence of wallpaper continues, the focus of this scheme is the wallpaper itself. Think of wallpaper as a large picture; if you can find a design you adore you'll probably never tire of it. If you have the budget or happen to be particularly artistic, you could design or commission a hand-painted wallpaper.

A clever combination of both modern and retro styles.

Find a striking wallpaper in rose-white (1) and grey clay (5) and use it on a feature wall in a lounge or dining room. Keep the remaining walls plain by painting in white clay (4), and choose a light, neutral floor covering so as not to overdo it.

For a touch of glamour, opt for modern or retro furniture and light fittings in barely black (2) with chrome (3) detailing. In a lounge, a sofa upholstered in fabulous grey clay fabric with rose-white (1) cushions will look fabulous.

Spring *white*

Choose springtime colours for a welcoming guest bedroom.

Quiet colours allow clarity of mind and will provide guests with a relaxing place to sleep. Don't overcrowd a guest bedroom, but think practically about what your visitors will need besides a bed: a dressing table or perhaps a chest of drawers, include a few hooks for hanging clothes and a good mirror.

1

2

3

Keep flooring bright with natural cotton (1), and mirror this colour in the furniture. For a subtle difference, paint the walls in lemon white (2) – the bright whites will reflect light around the room and create a feeling of space.

For a contemporary twist, paint a large, ornate framed mirror in warm stone (4), which will look great against the lemon white walls.

4

5

Add a simple Roman blind in a pattern of sandy stone (3) and rose stone (5) for a flash of colour, and finish with a vase of fresh roses on the dressing table.

Chocolate *truffle*

Smooth, velvety chocolate tones are neutral and inoffensive but warm and elegant at the same time. Here they are used as soft tints, subtle and understated yet instantly gratifying and welcoming. These colours would work anywhere, but are so incredibly inviting that they are ideal for a hallway.

A selection of soft chocolatey tones, perfect for a hallway.

1

2

3

Consider a striped paper in natural cotton (1) and chocolate milk (3) for a classic, elegant look for a hallway or grander entrance hall.

Apply deep skirting boards and paint any woodwork and stairs in pure white (4). Use a gorgeous, rich deep clay (5) carpet to give depth and lead the eye (and your guests!) through the space.

4

5

Accessorize with purple truffle (2) and natural cotton fabrics, and add a lantern or chandelier for a touch of glamour.

Vintage *modern*

Take inspiration from the past and combine old with new.

For a cool, serene and minimalist lounge, employ these gentle hues and use one-off designer or vintage pieces of furniture. Keep knicknacks to a bare minimum, and hide clutter away in streamlined, contemporary furniture.

1

2

3

4

5

Using a neutral backdrop of eggshell (1) painted walls, and add elegance and soft styling with a beautiful chaise lounge in bronze (3). To complement the vintage feel of the bronze finish, accessorize with cushions in citrus white (2) and iced blue (5) in varying textures of silks and cottons.

Keep flooring, whether carpet or wood boards, light and neutral in a light shade of eggshell.

For storage solutions choose a high-gloss, pure white (4) finish on doors and cabinets.

Warm *whites*

White is not only the most popular paint colour in the world but also the most complicated. There are simply hundreds of variations on the hue. Employ this scheme of warm whites in a space that has a double function, perhaps as a study and dining room.

Warm shades of white suit any surroundings.

1

2

3

Paper the dining area in eggshell (1) and stone white (2), while painting elsewhere in eggshell. These pale colours will give a spacious feel, while the paper defines a clear change of use.

Use a hard-wearing sisal flooring in deep clay (4) as another sound neutral base. Make dramatic floor-length drapes in the dining area and a simple Roman blind in the study section in soft iris (3) and white chocolate (5), defining the different areas but retaining the overall feel of space and unity.

4

5

Unusual *combinations*

Startling accents to punctuate an almost white interior.

For a neutral, calm living space, you don't have to stick to bleached-out colours and off-whites. The best interior designs work by unusual applications and quirky surprises within a flawless scheme.

1

2

3

Paint walls in subtle ivory (1) and all woodwork and ceilings in pure white (2). At the windows, hang thick, heavy cotton drapes in vanilla taupe (3) on chunky barely black (5) curtain poles.

4

5

Use buttercup (4) to upholster an unusual chair; bright and interesting colours will make a statement, but the overall feel of the scheme is neutral and light.

Use barely black for other items of furniture.

Into *the blue*

The colour of the sea and the sky, blue is a natural colour, fantastic at all levels of intensity. Its cool, calming effects make it an ideal shade for a bedroom, although the lighter, fresher versions included in this scheme will work well in any type of room.

A scheme that displays the restful, calming side of blue.

1

2

3

In a traditional room that can take a dado rail without cutting the room in two, try painting below the rail in the light shade of subtle ivory (1) and above it in a blue-green tone such as barely aqua (2).

4

For flooring use warm grey (5), the darkest shade, in a smart carpet or sisal matting. For furniture or upholstery use pure white (3) to evoke a clean-lined Scandinavian feel.

5

Accessorize with barely aqua and grey-blue (4) cushions and rugs to finish.

Elegant *white*

What cleaner and more refined colour is there than pure white?

While pure white can be impractical for a family environment, it has an amazing kudos within interior design. In most instances pure white is only used for ceilings and woodwork, but why not be ruthless and use it on all walls and architectural details?

1

2

3

Paint all walls, skirting boards, etc., in pure white (1). Keep the majority of furniture painted pure white also.

Finding a white carpet is almost impossible, so opt for off-white (3) instead.

4

5

White is so incredibly neutral that it really does go with any shade. Pick out particular objects for hints of colour, such as an oak chair with a sand (2) seat, a footstool in brown (5) or a warm cream (4) vase, and mix and match both colours and textures to your heart's content.

East *meets West*

Oriental influence in interior schemes has long graced our bedrooms and lounges. Inject your own taste of the Orient by combining a pure white base, with natural neutrals and dark woods for an elegant look that will work anywhere.

A basic yet timeless scheme inspired by the Orient.

1

2

3

In a lounge, hang pale pebble grey (3) curtains from elegant dark walnut (5) poles against pure white (1) coloured walls.

Sit a pair of clotted cream (2) sofas opposite each other, and dress with symmetrical dark taupe (4) cushions.

4

On a wood floor or plain carpet frame the sitting area with a dark taupe rug edged in clotted cream.

5

Accessorize with oversized dark-wood lamps with shades in clotted cream, and tall, dark floor vases placed in pairs.

Muted *tones*

A palette of refined colours for an entrance hall.

In a traditional setting, mixing up muted tones for fabrics, wallpapers and upholstery works extremely well. Combine tweeds, linens, cotton prints and patterned papers in these subdued tones for a stunning overall look.

1

2

3

In an entrance hall, paper with a substantial patterned paper in grey-white (1) and dove grey (2). Pair the paper with a traditional woven fabric in tones of juniper (4) and grey-white.

Select an area, perhaps up the stairs, to add simple tongue-and-groove panelling and paint in calico (3).

4

5

Finally, paint an old chest or console table in pearl (5) and top with a pair of elegant lamps with calico shades. If you have the space, you may want to re-cover an old easy chair in a shabby juniper fabric.

Built-in *luxury*

The heart of a home is often reputed to be the kitchen. With an increasing amount of our time centring around this room, it is important that we implement a thoughtful scheme. If you have an open-plan area you should choose clever storage and attractive finishes for the kitchen.

A selection of both lights and darks for a sleek kitchen.

Wash the room in simple grey-white (1) as a perfect base colour for the space.

Combine green oxide (2) and nickel (3) as finishes for kitchen units. Keep the nickel prominent, perhaps combining it with glass for super-sleek cupboards. Keep worktops bright, smart, clean and practical in pure white (4).

Finally, add hinted accessories in gorgeous pale aquamarine (5) for a cool, contemporary kitchen you'll want to show off.

Sun *blushed*

Fruity blushes heighten your appetite...

If you're lucky enough to have a large open-plan area, accent fruity reds, berry shades and warming whites with antiqued metallics for a luxurious atmosphere. In an open-air kitchen, even corners can be a cozy, practical living space.

To make the most of small or awkward spaces, use purpose-built fitted seating and add storage drawers or cupboards below them. Drench the walls with serene almond white (1), and upholster the seating area in bold eggplant (5). Paint any clever storage space the same colour as the walls so they blend into the background. Accessorize with cushions, vases, pictures and frames in old gold (2) and pewter (3), and use rich walnut (4) as a tone for accessories and occasional furniture, such as a nest of tables or a small bookshelf.